MY PEACOCK TALE

Secrets Of An NBC Page

By
Shelley Herman

BearManor Media.com

Typesetting and layout by BearManor Media

Published in the USA by
BearManor Media
P.O. Box 71436
Albany, GA 31708
www.BearManorMedia.com

Softcover Edition
ISBN-10:
ISBN-13: 979-8-88771-137-9

Published in the USA by Bear Manor Media

TABLE OF CONTENTS

ACKNOWLEDGMENTS

To my forever Band of Brothers and Sisters who worked at NBC Burbank including:

Emily Aiken, Alan Burnett, Dinah Brein, Tom Chasuk, Courtney Conte, Katherine Carter, Tim Danker, Paul Drinkwater, Billie Freebairn-Smith, Christine Gallagher, Jeff Garrett, George Gluvna, Pete Hammond, Cindy Hain, Tom Hansen, Linda (Levinson) Taylor, Lesa (Lindsay) Mattingly, Jeff Mackler, Marilee Mahoney, Jim McDonald, Gregg Moscoe, Al Ovadia, Renee Palyo, Tommy Patino, Maggie-Beth Rees, Brian Robinette, Sandy (Crompton) Selma, Neil Weiner, and Roxanne (Yamaguchi) Moster.

Additional thanks to the Page-In-Laws: Paul Brownstein, Daryl Busby, Randall Carver, Steve Goldstein, Madelyn Hammond, Larry McClellan, Todd Moster, Reggie Selma, Evan Swanson, Kathleen Swanson, Michele Walsh, and Linda Wilkes.

A special thank you to those whose kindness allowed me to use the letters and photos included in this book: Lisa D'Apolito, Howard Bragman, Michael Ratner, Susan Stafford, Jeff Sotzing, Jon Sotzing, and Alan Zweibel. And we remember the Pages who are no longer with us: Jill Brandt, Sue (Walsh) Brownstein, Jesse Gomez, and Tim Jones.

My thanks and gratitude to my friends from Agoura High School: James Michael Aldrin, Steve Carlson, Frank Esposito, James Gilchrist, Todd Jonz, Barb (Krivit) Meepos, Marty Meltzer, Joe Mesabi, Mike Mostakas, George O'Hanlon, Jr., Eileen (Daniel) Riddle, Terry Sciarrino, and Jeff White. And, another big thank you to my friends who are my safety net and my inspiration: Marla, Micki, Rachel, and Bob Boden, Cathy Hughart Dawson, Tom Edwards, Chad Eschman, Sharon Goldberg, Richard Hack, Karen Hartman, Mark Hess, Peter Marshall, Adam Nedeff, Susan Ruttan, Kathy Arntzen Roat & Richard Roat, Dr. Jay Silverman, and Janet Wood, Susan Shapiro, Marc Summers, Jess Walton, Fred Wostbrock, along with Andy Goldberg's Off the Wall Class and all the people I am privileged to work with, plus the talented writers and motivators in Margot Rose's Salon.

Finally, to my family, Lori, Christopher, and Marty Guerrero: I apologize for most of what you're about to read ahead of time.

INTRODUCTION

The bookmobile pulled into the semi-circular driveway at A.E. Wright Elementary School in Calabasas, and we were told we had to select a book to read. At that moment, it dawned on me this was the first time I was able to choose a book to read all by myself. I thumbed through a few books, and it was daunting. I knew what a prince was, but I didn't know what a pauper was. *The Legend of Sleepy Hollow* looked interesting, but I couldn't figure out how to pronounce Ichabod Crane, yet alone what an Ichabod Crane was. Then I saw the book I wanted to read, a biography of Jacqueline Kennedy.

The cover was made from a royal blue cloth; the lettering was gold. It had that library book smell, a little musty with a touch of gravitas. Other people must have read this book and gained knowledge; now, it was my turn. I devoured the book in one sitting. Did you know that when Jackie was First Lady, she had people iron her nylon stockings and bed sheets? Yeah, that was my takeaway.

Since then, I have loved to hear real-life stories.

Whenever two or more NBC Pages are gathered, a Memory Storm emerges. Stories, good and bad and insane, begin flowing from our communal psyches. The overwhelming sentiment is what a great time we had and that if we could, we'd do it all again. Former NBC President Brandon Tartikoff was correct when he titled his autobiography, *The Last Great Ride*. My time, especially this time at NBC Burbank, was the tail end of an era that gave us some of the greatest stars and personalities in television history. It will never be duplicated or eclipsed. I grew up watching programs like *The Tonight Show Starring Johnny Carson, Laugh-In, Bob Hope Specials,* and *Hollywood Squares*. And now, I was going to be a part of the NBC family, where I could live and breathe television history as it was happening.

My sincere thanks to my NBC Page colleagues for their stories. Some names have been changed, but all the events are true.

Chapter One

HOW I GOT TO WHERE I GOT TO

You never know how it's going to happen. Little did I know, nor could I have imagined, that when I took a thankless job, it would lead me to get my foot in the door for my dream job as a Page at the NBC Studios in Burbank.

I was the quintessential theater kid at Agoura High School, in what was, at the time, a rural community located about thirty miles from Hollywood. The teachers weren't much older than the students. Creativity was encouraged, and we were taught the skills to practice our craft, and the freedom to think beyond our little dirt-covered campus.

While in high school, I worked as a Salad Bar Hostess at The People Tree Inn, off Las Virgenes Road, the only nice steakhouse in the area. Dressed in my skort (a combination of a skirt and shorts) and my white knee-high boots, it was my job to refill the containers in the salad bar. To this day, I'm not fond of pickled beets or marinated artichoke hearts. Occasionally, I'd see some teachers at the tables and slip them free drinks, so it was fun and I could act like a grown-up on Friday and Saturday nights.

It was a tough choice, but, being a theater kid at heart, I traded working in a smoke-filled restaurant/bar (where I was getting patted on the ass nightly by the regulars) for the pivotal role of Helen Keller when I got cast in our high school's production of *The Miracle Worker.*

After graduation, I managed to sponge off my parents, as long as I went to college. I took a part-time job as a salesgirl in the Junior Bazaar department at Sears in Canoga Park to start saving for a car. I attended California State University at Northridge by day and sold clothes that smelled like popcorn by night. It was an awful job, as most of the customers were slobs who left their discarded clothes piled on the dressing room floors. I had to rehang the clothes, which was no easy task as I had to figure out which polyester piece went on each lookalike unfashionable rack. Sears was known for their Craftsman brand tools, not its fashion sense. The clothes were so itchy and ugly that we rarely had a problem with shoplifters. One day, I went to management to suggest they no longer carry a particular maternity blouse with tiny images that read, "I'm a Happy Hippo." Yeah, it was that kind of place.

I usually worked a shift alongside Janus, a quiet, plain girl who wore braces the entire year and a half I knew her. She lived within walking distance of Sears and often arrived at work looking a little sweaty with stringy hair. I've always had a soft spot for the people who get overlooked by others, and I would offer to drive her home at night. We never really talked much, just exchanged pleasantries, until one night, she floated the idea that we get a group of our fellow sales gals together to see Elvis in Las Vegas. I thought, yeah, sure, Elvis. How could we get tickets or even afford a hotel on a Sears salary?

It turns out her dad, not an Elvis fan, had sold the rock icon a couple of television sets. I remember hearing Elvis would sometimes take aim and shoot the picture tube out of a television set if he didn't like something he saw, so it made sense. Elvis comped Janus' dad with five tickets to his show...and a weekend at the Hilton International Hotel. As you can imagine, Janus didn't have to ask any of the sales gals twice. So, off we went: Mary-Marie and the two Susans piled in one car while Janus and I hit the road in my recently purchased used 1975 yellow Toyota Corona. It didn't matter that it didn't have air conditioning because we were young and stupid and didn't care.

Mary-Marie, a gangly, tomboyish brunette towered over all of us at a little over six feet tall, had another agenda while in Vegas. She wanted to lose her virginity. Mary-Marie was tired of being a good Catholic schoolgirl. To make her escape to Sin City, she told her mom she'd be staying at a friend's house. Fueled by weed, Boone's Farm Apple Wine, and the two Susans' sage advice, Mary-Marie was going to make sure her virginity stayed in Vegas. The two Susans were almost identical blondes who knew how to have a good time (and had the hickeys to prove it.)

We pulled into the valet parking area of the Hilton International Hotel as the bellhop retrieved our juvenile-looking luggage. Mary-Marie and the two Susans in one room, Janus and I in the smaller room. We changed into our evening attire, trying our best to look at least twenty-one years old so we could order drinks. And it worked, because we were escorted to the best seats in the house, ringside. And yes, I was able to place my order for my two-drink minimum: the newly fashionable Tequila Sunrise.

The lights dimmed, the music played, and out walked Jackie Kahane, Elvis' opening act. Jackie was working the room like he was the headliner. And no one cared. I felt terrible for him. Twenty long minutes later, he took a bow. The lights dimmed. The music swelled as the theme to "*2001: A Space Odyssey*" filled the room. You could feel the energy as the audience sat up in their seats. The brass section was wailing to the beat of "*See, See Rider.*" The crowd was now on their feet, the applause thunderous. Women began rushing the stage and rushing us as we grabbed our drinks and hoped for the best.

After what seemed like an eternity, there he was. Elvis! Wearing what I'd hoped to see him in: a heavily bedazzled white jumpsuit with a detachable cape. He took long strides, walking back and forth several times across the stage, then stopped, right in front of us, undulating his hips, posing in all the signature Elvis karate moves, smiling a bright white smile. His jet-black hair was already glistening with sweat, and once we got over our initial shock of witnessing Elvis up close, we did notice he had put on a few pounds.

As he sang, women lined the apron of the stage, laying their gifts at the feet of Elvis. Some had posters, and one had a giant turquoise squash-blossom necklace. Elvis, wearing different colorful silk scarves, would pat his forehead and bend down to his adoring fans as they slowly removed the scarf from the neck of their idol. He gave every fan their moment and never dropped a note or forgot a lyric, even with all the distractions.

I grew up listening to The Beatles, and Elvis wasn't really on my radar. Don't get me wrong; I liked him in films like *Viva Las Vegas* and *Blue*

Hawaii. As a live performer, Elvis didn't disappoint. I had a renewed respect for his talent as a showman and that voice! He sang all the hits, and the fans couldn't get enough. What a love-fest! I still get goosebumps (and a bit teary) when I hear his rendition of "*In the Ghetto.*" We stayed as long as they'd allow us, sitting in the best seats in the house, until the house announcer said those five famous words: "Elvis has left the building."

What a night! We were a bit buzzed and high on the whole Elvis Experience. Still on the prowl, Mary-Marie caught the eye of a great-looking guy in the theater lobby, and before I could say, "Where should we go next," Mary-Marie was gone. We were all happy for her because even if her mystery man were a lousy lay, she could dream of Elvis. The two Susans ditched Janus and me to gamble and party, leaving me with Janus. It was getting close to midnight, and I was ready to hit the strip, but Janus was tired and wanted to go back to the room.

I felt terrible for her. She'd set up the whole weekend, and the other girls ditched her. I tried to persuade Janus to do some sightseeing, but we only got as far as the coffee shop, where we had warm cherry pie with vanilla ice cream. I guess that old saying is correct: You can take the girl out of Sears, but you can't take the Sears out of the girl.

It was too cold to sit by the pool, and I was too broke to have any real fun, so Janus and I hung around the hotel, did some people-watching, and had a few meals together. We were getting to know each other, and she opened up to me that she'd had a hard life. Her parents had a messy divorce, so this grand gesture on her dad's part, this weekend with her friends, meant the world to her. I was the only person she could share her feelings with, as the other girls were nowhere in sight. At that moment, I knew I was in the place I was supposed to be.

We didn't see Mary-Marie again until we checked out of the hotel two days later. She got out of a convertible and kissed the same hot-looking guy we saw after the Elvis concert. She walked, no, glided toward the valet area carrying a new designer purse, wearing a few new pieces of jewelry, smiling the smile of a woman whose road trip to womanhood was not detoured. I felt slightly left out when Mary-Marie and the two

Susans took off in one car, and I was stuck driving home with Janus in my Toyota. I was dying to get all the juicy details of Mary-Marie's obviously fabulous weekend.

I would love to tell you Mary-Marie's romance had a happy ending, but I would be remiss if I didn't tell you what happened about a month after our road trip. Early one morning, Mary-Marie's mother answered the front door of her home, only to be greeted by two men bearing FBI badges. They had photos taken from security cameras at various casinos of Mary-Marie and the man we saw her with, who turned out to be a bank robber laundering his loot in Las Vegas. Mary-Marie was busted by her mom *and* the FBI, who confiscated her new purse and jewelry as evidence.

All our time in Las Vegas did give Janus and me more time to bond. She was uncertain about her future, but I was laser-focused on becoming an NBC Page. I told Janus that I went to the tapings of the TV series *The Midnight Special* and *The Tonight Show* when I was in high school and saw a bunch of people wearing uniforms, ushering for the shows, giving tours of the building, and thought I could do that!

I had written countless letters trying to get an interview for a coveted spot in the Page Program, long recognized as one of the premier gateways to a career in the entertainment industry. My family isn't in show biz, and I didn't know anyone who could slip my letter and meager résumé to the top of the Human Resources pile. Janus casually mentioned that her mom's best friend worked at NBC, and she'd see what she could do to help. Much to my complete surprise, Janus asked her mom's friend, Jean Messerschmitt, a longtime NBC employee, to meet me at Sears. Jean called the legendary Eba Hawkins, Head of the Page Staff, and my interview was all set. Eba was a formidable woman with a booming voice and a passion for golf and brown cigarettes. Janus's simple act of kindness gave me the opportunity I longed for, and (spoiler alert), I got the job! I had two weeks before my training at NBC began, so I took my entire savings ($550), bought a round-trip ticket on Pan Am Airlines, and went to London by myself for a week.

How was I to know that trip would become the setting for an unexpected and unforgettable life lesson this newly anointed Page would ever learn?

I had always been envious of my friends whose families would travel to Europe for their summer vacation. My family liked to go camping. To me, it was a kidnapping, and I hated every moment of it. I wanted to see the world, walk in the steps of Shakespeare, take in the shows at the West End, drink warm beer...but I guess I could have had a warm beer while camping. I wanted to make the most out of my week, as I was sure it would be the last vacation I'd be able to take in a long time. After all, my foot was in the door, and I was going to be working non-stop in show biz!

My parents dropped me off at LAX, and I promised to call them when I got to the hotel. I was instructed to do the old trick some people used to do to avoid a long-distance phone charge. I'd place a collect call to the long-distance operator, who would dial my home and ask for "Shelley Herman." My mother would decline the call, now knowing I was safe, and it wouldn't cost her a cent. I got on the plane, grabbed a pillow and blanket, and snagged a window seat. I don't know why I got a pillow and blanket. I was so excited, and there was no way I would be able to sleep. I immediately introduced myself to my row mate, a good-looking guy traveling on business to a studio in England. He was a genuinely nice guy and asked if I wanted to watch him work on a movie, but I politely declined, explaining I was already in "the business" and I'd be hanging around a lot of studios once I got home. There was also a red-haired man who caught my eye. Not in a romantic way, more like in an I-wonder-if-he's-related-to-Jack-the-Ripper way.

Throughout my week across the pond, I would see the red-haired man daily, and I'd nod and smile at him as I toured London, Oxford, and Stratford-Upon-Avon. A friend of mine asked me if I could do her a favor by going to Harrod's Department store to get her elderly British mom a box of their chocolate-dipped oranges, a mission I gladly accomplished. My former high school theatre teacher, Jim Gilchrist, also asked a favor of me. He told me to go to the Tom Cribb Pub, look for "two very old people" seated at the end of the bar, and tell them Jimmy from America says hi and buy them drinks. Sure enough, they were sitting where he told me they'd be, she in her white crocheted gloves, he three sheets to the wind. They looked like two little toothless pickled people, with faces resembling withered, apple-headed dolls. I couldn't understand a word they were saying, so, as Jim suggested, I just smiled a nodded. I was having a great time traveling alone. I saw five plays in five days and was invited to a private club by a few new Brits I'd met. I got a loud, continuous bout of the hiccups on Shakespeare's grave, got rid of them with warm beer, and purchased a bone china tea set (which, to this day, I've never used). Oh, and I did get to witness Queen Elizabeth II's 25th Jubilee celebration, so that was fun and splendidly British. I was now the embodiment of all free-spirited, single ladies I saw on television and read about in Ms. Magazine. As I boarded the flight home, I saw the red-haired man again. I'd never been accused of being shy, so I extended my hand and remarked that it was about time we officially met. He said, "My name is Korn," and proceeded to spell it out, "K-O-R-N." I said, "Oh, there is a character in the novel *Catch-22* named Colonel Korn, and he replied, "Yes, I have been meaning to look him up to see if we're related."

I didn't want to break his heart and tell him the book was a work of fiction, so I just moved on.

The 747 took off, and I buckled up for the long flight home, imbued with a new spirit and purpose. I was going to throw myself into my new job. I would become the career woman who could have it all. I promised myself that when I retired, I would travel more. No sooner did I have that thought, a little over halfway across the Atlantic Ocean, and while watching the in-flight movie, Alfred Hitchcock's *Family Plot*, an old guy near the back of the plane got up to use the restroom, keeled over, and passed out cold!

It didn't take long for the cabin crew to respond. The first message, spoken by a female flight attendant with a crisp British accent, came over the loudspeaker asking if a doctor was on board. Well, K-O-R-N stood up, along with a few other men, and announced he was a doctor! "What kind of doctor are you?" I asked. "A dermatologist," he replied. I thought the old guy didn't faint because of a rash, but at least Dr. Korn offered his assistance. The following message from the same flight attendant was something out of a Monty Python skit: "Ladies and Gentleman, I know this is an indelicate question, but does anyone onboard have a douchebag?" I am assuming a doctor wanted to intubate the poor man lying in the aisle by inserting the tube attached to the douchebag down his throat. Next, the flight attendant, now sounding like Monty Hall on *Let's Make a Deal*, wanted to know if anyone had a tennis ball on them. I assume it would be used as a makeshift hand pump attached to the douchebag hose to aerate his airway. All this took place while the flicker of the Hitchcock film was playing on the wall-sized screen, illuminating the cabin.

Word quickly spread that the man was unresponsive. An older woman was sobbing loudly, and the flight crew did their best to console her. The pilot declared an emergency, and our plane was diverted to a Canadian Air Force Base in Goose Bay, a province of Newfoundland and Labrador. The crew needed to find a coroner to pronounce the man dead so his body could be removed from the plane. But it was the coroner's night off, so after waiting for three hours on the ground, the older man was placed into two extra-large dark green garbage bags, one over his head, another started at his feet, covering his legs, and was tucked into his waistband. He was laid out in the back row of seats next to his grieving companion, secured by seat belts. We flew to Chicago's O'Hare International Airport and cleared customs in record time.

I raced for the payphone to call my parents, who had agreed to pick me up at LAX. I didn't want to do the old collect call trick because I needed to explain to them someone had died on the plane, and it wasn't me. I told them to please check the updated arrival time, as I had no idea what was happening. While waiting for a flight back to LA, I ran into the first man I'd met on the plane to England and asked him how his movie was coming along.

He said, "Great, something really extraordinary," and I should keep my eye out for it when it comes out next year.

"What's the title?" I asked.

"*Star Wars*", *h*e replied.

Yep, I chose the Tower Bridge Tour over *Star Wars*, and yes, I still regret it.

Why this story? Because, at the ripe old age of twenty, I thought I knew it all. I had a plan, a sure-fire career path. I would be an NBC Page, quickly get promoted, get a better position, and write what was destined to be a classic television show. I'd run the network, win numerous awards, then retire and become a respected political advisor and philanthropist. That all changed the second that older man died on the plane. It was as though I had a seismic shift in my psyche. I realized I didn't want to be that all-work-and-no-play person. I didn't want to wait 45 years to have fun. I made the conscious choice to say yes to opportunities, to talk to people—better still, to listen to people, and learn what to do and what not to do.

It turns out my biggest life lesson came from a dead man.

Wait to retire? Hell no. Let the adventures begin!

Chapter Two

WHAT IS A PAGE?

Welcome to the NBC Tour. Before we begin our tour, there can be no smoking, drinking, eating, or taking pictures.

There has always been a mystique surrounding The NBC Page Program. Established in 1933 in New York and 1936 in Los Angeles, it is considered one of the most prestigious executive training programs available to college graduates looking to work in the television industry. Not everyone hired becomes the next network honcho. One famous Page who never received a key to the executive washroom was the late Regis Philbin. He holds the Guinness World Record for the most hours (over 16,746) on US television. Regis beat the long-standing record of venerable newsman Hugh Downs, also former NBC Page. High school student Bob Keeshan, best remembered as the title character portrayed on the children's show *Captain Kangaroo* gave tours in New York before he began his tour of duty in the Marines. (Sidebar: When I was a kid, I thought the man who played Captain Kangaroo and Walter Cronkite were the same person. Both had white hair and a mustache. My kid's logic thought the man would dress as a Captain in the morning and talk to children, and then dress up in a suit and talk to adults.) TV personalities Peter Marshall, Gene Rayburn, Chuck Barris, Aubrey Plaza, and Richard Benjamin were not only Pages; they went on to star in NBC television series. In the early days of the program, Peter Marshall told me they were referred to as "Page Boys." No women were allowed to join their ranks. In a full-circle moment, Peter's daughter Jamie joined our little Pagedom in the late 1970s.

Since I worked at the 3000 West Alameda, Burbank, California facility, the company was sold several times and is now known as NBCUniversal. The East Coast location is at 30 Rockefeller Center in New York, immortalized in Tina Fey's comedy series, *30 Rock.* It's also home to

Saturday Night Live, The Tonight Show Starring Jimmy Fallon, Late Night with Seth Meyers, The Today Show, and *NBC Nightly News.*

The modern era program had changed considerably, as I learned when I spoke to former Page, current Vice President, Talent, Early Career at NBCUniversal, Christina Noval. NBCU recruits college graduates two or three times a year and receives about 16,000 applications for this prestigious program. Only about two percent of applicants make the final cut. People who do math better than I do have that calculated the odds of getting accepted to Harvard are better than becoming an NBC Page. The Page staff numbers about ninety people in New York and about fifty in Universal City, CA. They're all full-time employees who are given medical and dental benefits, along with vacation and sick days.

Noval emphasized the ongoing efforts to make the program inclusive: "We have also created a large stipend for new Pages who start with us. We recognize not everyone can hop on a plane and get an apartment rather quickly, or have the financial resources to get themselves started in the city. We're really hoping to make the program more accessible. The Pages are such a big part of our history. We want to make sure they have everything they need."

Pages are now given twelve months to complete three assignments, each lasting four months in different divisions of NBCU. The New York Pages, in addition to giving tours and working with audiences who attend the taping of TV shows, have many opportunities to work in the sports, sales, and news divisions, whereas the West Coast Pages do their rotations in the more entertainment-oriented divisions. Sadly, the West Coast Pages no longer give tours, as that is already a function of the Universal City Studios Tour operation. In addition to their rotations, Pages will be brought in for special events.

Both staffs are able to work special events. When their twelve months are up, they have, in effect, graduated from the program. They then have an additional four months during which they are encouraged to look for jobs within NBCU.

Noval continued, "We have the Pages doing supplemental assignments, helping them with their job search. We're coaching them, doing lots of workshops with them prepping for that launch, hopefully, into roles at the company."

So, how did my friends get their jobs? We were a diverse staff of male and female, Black, Asian, and Hispanic, and straight and gay Pages in our ranks. Having a college degree helped a lot, and like so many jobs, having good references did, too. Some, like Neil Weiner, called Eba Hawkins every week. Because of his persistence, Neil got the job the day after graduating from USC. Some people had family connections, like Pete Hammond, who blew his first opportunity to be a Page big time. His mother knew someone who knew someone who knew former NBC President Julian Goodman.

Eba brought Pete in right away, explained the job, and Pete replied, "I don't want to be a Page. They just sent me down here. I want to work in the news business." A year later, desperate for work, Pete was able to sneak into an NBC event at the Century Plaza Hotel and meet Julian Goodman face-to-face. Goodman wrote a letter to Eba, who, thankfully, had forgotten their first meeting. Pete walked into his interview as it were the first time, wearing a homemade button on his lapel inspired by the peace movement that read, "All We Are Saying Is Give Pete A Chance." The job was his.

Tommy Patino was giving tours on the Queen Mary, docked in Long Beach, CA. After his tour, he was approached by someone who complimented him on his abilities and asked if he had ever thought of becoming an NBC Page. "Thought of it. Only in my dreams. I didn't know anyone who could get me in." This guy got him an interview, and he was in!

Former Seattle ladies' shoe salesman Al Ovadia became a contestant on the NBC daytime game show *Wheel of Fortune*. He noticed the Pages and began asking how he could get a job doing what they were doing. Now, the story I'd always heard was that Al, with his thick head of black hair, azure blue eyes, and warm smile, was enthusiastically recruited by both the female and male Pages to join their ranks. Either way, he got the job and received a promotion within twelve weeks of his start date.

Somehow, I was the exception to many of the rules, but I got the job anyway. I was twenty years old, still in my junior year of college, and carrying a full class load at California State University, Northridge. As you read this book and stumble through my attempts at correct sentence structure, you'll see I had no chance of getting into Harvard. My only previous experience in the ushering business was volunteering during the summer at The Valley Music Theater in Woodland Hills, California. It was an enormous white-domed structure that never lived up to the community's expectations as an elegant theatre in the round. I ushered on Aisle One, where the VIPs were seated. The highlight of my brief tenure was when I linked arms with Jack Benny and Groucho Marx, helping them to their seats to see Woody Allen perform stand-up comedy.

When I became a Page, I wasn't put through any formal training program. I studied the history of NBC so I could be prepared for any questions I might be asked. As the newest recruits, we would shadow the veteran Pages to hear what they said on their tours. We would observe how the Pages worked as a crew, ushering guests into the building to see game shows and situation comedies, all taped before a live studio audience. This is how we learned everything we needed to know to be assigned to the best gig on the lot: *The Tonight Show Starring Johnny Carson.*

When I mentioned to a few of my longtime Page friends that I wanted to share their stories about our time walking the halls in Burbank, Renee Palyo called. She told me she'd found her husband Tim Jones' NBC Page Manual. (Yes, they met as Pages!) When Renee offered it to me, I shrieked, "You found the Holy Grail!" I had never heard of, let alone seen, any official manual when I began. Yet, there it was. I gently opened the pristine three-ringed binder and was greeted with a bizarre sketch of a Page drawn by singer Dean Martin's nephew, Guy Crocetti. What a blast from the past! I was immediately transported back to June 21, 1976, the Longest Day in the Northern Hemisphere, and my first official day as an NBC Page.

Our eighteen-month NBC Page Program could be considered a post-graduate program that pays you. Once a Page had their foot in the door, it was up to them to maximize their opportunities and meet people with the hope of moving up the corporate ladder. If you were one of the lucky Pages, you might be given temporary assignments in different departments as vacation relief where they could get a feel for working full-time at the network level.

Before a new Page could eventually take over the network, we were obligated to be NBC's Ambassadors. Primarily, this meant giving tours of the 43-acre facility and ushering guests when TV shows had a live audience. We were the first contact the guests would have with the network, so it was up to us to ensure the visit met their expectations and was a positive experience. That was often easier said than done, especially when none of the stages were open, no stars were around, and no shows were taping. Thankfully, by listening to other Pages who had read our manual, I was able to gather enough useless trivia to haul a group of people around for an hour so they could get their money's worth. Some fascinating facts included the following:

The NBC audio chimes are in the key of C, and the musical notes are G, E, and C. At the time, General Electric Corporation owned NBC. Coincidence or folklore?

The NBC Peacock first appeared in 1956, months before we began broadcasting programs that were "brought to you in Living Color." On game shows like *Hollywood Squares*, celebrities had to bring five changes of clothes but only had to change from the waist up, as they were always seated in the Tic-Tac-Toe designed set (complete with spiral staircases, for a quick escape in case of an earthquake). Each "square" had individual lighting and speakers. And, in true Hollywood style, each star had a fan in the square. It wasn't a person. It was to keep the talent from sweating. (That was a joke, folks.)

NBC's monthly power bill was about $42,000. The talent worked under 10,000 watts of lamps that could heat the studio to 120 °F in 7 – 10 minutes. NBC spent about $4,000 a month on all different sizes of light bulbs. The total cost of the light bulbs used to spell out the logo for Midnight Special was $63,000.

We'd talk about how the *Days of Our Lives* set was shaped like a horseshoe so the cameras could move freely. The tours were never allowed on their stage, located in a separate building in an area nicknamed The Back 40. It was also a place where some Pages got high.

Can you guess the longest-running show on NBC? It is *Meet the Press,* which premiered in 1947.

The floor tiles were rented for $0.75 each. (Yes, we even talked about floor tiles!)

At the start of the tour route, we pointed out an iconic prop, safely protected behind Plexiglas: The Fickle Finger of Fate Award, made famous on the comedy/variety series *Rowan & Martin's Laugh-In.* We never had anything as fabulous as the shark from *Jaws* to show the tourists. We did have a special effect meant to wow the crowd, a fog machine that spewed smoke from a never-ending supply of oil that I'm sure caused our current climate crisis.

Once inside the facility, we'd wax poetic about the large portals used to bring the sets on and off the stage, and the metal doors that were closed while shows taped. They're called Elephant Doors, and in all my years at NBC Burbank, I never saw anyone bring an elephant onto the stage. After two o'clock, when most shows began rehearsing or taping, we'd say, "If you could see behind these elephant doors..."

We'd talk about cue cards, the junk on the set of *Sanford and Son,* and the approximate cost of everything-from sets stored in the hallways to wardrobe to show budgets-because we never knew the correct amounts, and people seemed satisfied with our answers anyway.

Tom Chasuk lamented that he had trouble giving a full one-hour tour on weekends when almost every stage was closed. He said he got so desperate for facts he would tell everyone (who was still paying attention) that this was the vending machine where the stars buy their apples and oranges. Roxanne (Yamaguchi) Moster gave her tour group an extra thrill when, while walking backward, she fell, and her skirt flew up over her blazer! One of the guys on the tour broke the tension and got a huge laugh when he said, "Are you sure we can't take any pictures on this tour?"

Let's face it. Most people took the NBC Tour to get a glimpse of a star. Thank goodness for Floyd! Floyd Jackson began shining shoes for the stars at NBC Burbank in 1951, and before he came west, he had his first glimpse of a movie star when he shined John Wayne's boots. That's a set-up at the upscale Rice Hotel in Houston, Texas. It's there he had when Floyd got the idea to move to Hollywood. He packed up his portable shoeshine stand and started making the rounds of studios, meeting clients where they worked at facilities, including Warner Brothers, MGM, Universal, and ABC.

Floyd finally found a permanent home for his stand at NBC Burbank, which he located outside Studio 1, in the line of sight of all the arriving guests appearing on *The Tonight Show*. Floyd took a great deal of pride in his work. He made it a point to go to Johnny's dressing room every day before the show. He wanted to make sure Johnny's shoes were shining when he stepped center stage on the white star to begin his monologue.

Floyd was the best tour time-killer in the whole facility! He was always good for a story or two (or three). The walls behind his stand were covered with autographed photos from dozens of NBC stars he'd known over the decades. I'm proud to say I was one of the Pages who had their picture taken with Floyd for some promotional purpose. A poster-sized copy of the photo-which includes my dear friends to this day, Dinah Brein, Pete Hammond, and Jim McDonald-hangs in my office. When I asked Tom Hansen what he remembered about this iconic photo, he told me, "Jim McDonald ran into the commissary and said they needed a bunch of Pages for a photo. That's how Risé Irushalmi and I got in the photo." It was his first day as a Page in uniform.

Floyd's daily routine involved going to the offices of the NBC Executives. If requested, he would collect their shoes early in the morning, then return them as quickly as possible. The rest of the afternoon, he'd be available to all the other employees, who would often bring their friends to Floyd's-both for a shine and for a moment to chat with the legend himself. Many stars saw it as a bit of good luck to have Floyd shine their shoes before they performed.

Floyd had his own taste of TV stardom, too. Bob Barker asked him to do a bit on the game show *Truth or Consequences*. Since Laugh-In was taped down the hall, Don Rickles grabbed him for a quick comedy sketch appearing as, well, Floyd, The Shoeshine Man. Floyd finally appeared as a guest on *The Tonight Show*, plugging an extremely short book he'd written about shining star's shoes. David Letterman interviewed him, too. He even posed for photos with circus animals. Everyone liked Floyd!

His best story involved his A-list tippers. Sammy Davis, Jr. gave him a $10 tip and told him to buy a turkey for his family. That was followed by Frank Sinatra giving Floyd a $50 gratuity, jokingly telling him to buy two turkeys and a ham.

When Floyd wasn't there to tell it himself, the story we all told also involved Frank Sinatra. Frank hopped into one of the chairs while Floyd shined his shoes.

Satisfied with a job well done, Frank asked, "What's the biggest tip you ever received?"

Floyd answered immediately, "Well, Mr. Sinatra, it was $100." So Frank reached into his pocket and gave Floyd $101.

Frank then asked, "Who gave you the $100 tip?" Floyd, smiling, replied, "You did, Mr. Sinatra!"

Opera Superstar Placido Domingo gave Floyd a $99 tip, with good reason. Floyd said, "He was getting a shine, and an NBC tour came by. I told them about Frank giving me $100.

When Placido got off the stand, he said, 'Floyd, give me a dollar.' So I gave him a dollar, and he handed me a $100 bill. Domingo said, 'Me and Frank are very good friends, and I don't want to out-tip Frank.'"

He had stories about practically every star in town, from TV pioneers like Bob Hope to the then-President of NBC, Brandon Tartikoff, who once joked, "Floyd Jackson is the only person who knows what it's like to be in my shoes."

Floyd retired in 1981. As a tribute, his workplace remained the same and was a popular fixture on tour. The photos surrounding the stand made it a fun place to stop and reminisce about the good ol' days. Floyd believed that "Show people are the greatest people on earth. I just love them. I think about it, and you know I never heard of a shine man being a star. I'm not bragging about it, but I made my own self a star."

One tourist left Neil Weiner absolutely speechless midway through his tour. Our normal route took us to the right, and we'd circle through the set construction area, past the wardrobe department, up to Studios 1 and 3, past the local KNBC News Studio, then on to Studios 2 – 4, before finally bidding our group of twenty-ish people bye-bye from NBC Burbank. On days we were swamped with tours, we would sometimes reverse the order of the tour so we wouldn't overlap with other clusters of guests. Neil was in the middle of saying something when a woman put her hand down her blouse, exposing her breast as she began to nurse the infant in her arms. The unflappable Neil was flapped, and he told me, "I was totally speechless! I tried to remember what I had said, which way we began the tour. I started to repeat myself. I was completely shocked!"

So, you get the idea. It could be grim trying to come up with stuff to talk about to hold a tour group's interest. Former Page Katherine Carter recalled how one of the Pages would tell the crowd he was sorry they wouldn't be able to look into Studio 5P, the local news studio, because it was filled with water and is being used for the Lloyd Bridges series *Sea Hunt*. It never occurred to anyone that this was a lie because *Sea Hunt* went off the air in 1961.

At the end of the tour, we would ask the group if they had any questions. Inevitably, they'd want to know how to get tickets to *The Tonight Show*. Keep in mind NBC Burbank was an authentic working studio, not a specially designed tourist attraction. We welcomed about 150,000 people a year on tours, and nearly one million more who attended the taping of TV shows. On an average day, I would give three to four tours, then race over to a TV taping.

I loved being in the room where it happened, watching people I had only seen on TV, live, doing their thing as actors, hosts, or charming game show personalities. It's where someone's dream, plus countless hours of preparation, meets imagination and is finally realized. Even now, I never get blasé when I think of those days.

Our iconic uniforms were 100% polyester. We wore blue blazers with the NBC logo on the left side over our hearts. The women wore white blouses with an attached scarf that could be tied into a pussy bow or worn like an ascot, and gray pleated skirts. The men wore a white collared shirt, a tie, and gray pleated slacks. The uniforms were dry-cleaned weekly by NBC, which was great because I was broke. I washed my blouse in the sink at home if it was getting too ripe. Only one guy I worked with, Courtney Conte, refused to wear the regulation polyester pants. Instead, he'd wear his own wool trousers. The women needed to wear nylons, not tights. And we were told we must wear black or navy blue closed-toed shoes. I readily admit I violated that policy on more than a few occasions. Let's face it, after a long day on the job walking on cement floors, my feet hurt! Frequently, I would get busted for wearing my Easy Spirit sandals. We were prohibited from chewing gum and were advised not to eat onions or garlic at lunch or dinner. We were also told to always have these three things in our blazer pocket: a pen, breath mints, and a lighter (because people still smoked back then). So, there you have it: Pagedom.

Many of my colleagues told me that being a member of the Page staff was like being in a fraternity or sorority-and, if they could, they'd do it all again. True Confession: At the end of my final shift working *The Tonight Show*, I stole my uniforms and shoved them into my purse on my way out the door. I still have them neatly stored in a garment bag. I consider them, as they say in the game show biz, lovely parting gifts.

Chapter Three

ALWAYS IN THE HALLWAYS

CBs, OICs, and DFs

Many times our tours would stop outside the hallways in the faint hope of seeing a star. The best chances for this were usually after lunch when the technical crew had finished loading in the scenery and setting the lights. Most of the time, you could catch a glimpse of a celebrity doing one of the numerous game shows that were always taping at the facility, including *Hollywood Squares, Password,* or *Celebrity Sweepstakes.* Bob Hope would tape his variety specials a few times a year. For one season, *Dick Clark's Live Wednesday* was a genuinely live show from Burbank filled with eclectic acts, and an infamous fall-down-some-stairs by Suzanne Somers. If you wanted to meet celebrities in an unguarded moment, the hallways were the place to be.

The first celebrity I saw up close and in person was Janet Leigh, best remembered for her shower scene in the Alfred Hitchcock classic film *Psycho* and as the mother of actress Jamie Lee Curtis. I didn't recognize her at first. Janet was shockingly tiny in height and weight. Her hair was wrapped in a flowing scarf, and she was wearing dark glasses, all signs of a star, except she was carrying a garment bag that was quite heavy. I quickly took it from her as we walked to her dressing room. It wasn't until I saw her name neatly typed on a card inserted into a holder on her dressing room door that I knew it was Janet. Her voice was unmistakable as she thanked me for the help. An hour later, the Janet Leigh I knew, with a teased hairdo, fully made up with a smart-looking blouse, emerged from her dressing room ready to play *Hollywood Squares.*

Show biz icons were always roaming the hallways when *Hollywood Squares,* hosted by former NBC Page Peter Marshall, was taping. I had a fun encounter with Vincent Price, who was such a gentleman. I walked over to him and said, as a young girl, I saw him play Captain Hook in a live theatrical production of *Peter Pan*. Vincent would skulk through the audience, brandishing his hook, laughing manically, frightening the children. When I told him how much he'd scared me, he replied, with a twinkle in his eye, "Good, I was doing my job."

On my way to the Subterranean Page Lounge, located downstairs between Studios 1 and 3, to change from my street clothes into my uniform, I walked past Academy Award-winning actress Patty Duke who was wearing the same brown peasant blouse I was wearing.

Patty looked at me and said, "You remind me of me."

I replied, "Like identical cousins?"

For a moment, I feared my little joke referencing her dual role on "The Patty Duke Show" fells flat, but she threw her head back and laughed, along with her husband, actor John Astin.

Of everyone I saw in the hallways, only one person took my breath away. She walked the walk of a dancer, gliding between Studios 2 and 4 on her way to guest-star on a *Bob Hope Special*. She was wearing a bright green chiffon dress with a high slit up the side. Her legs were stunning and so long. I looked to see who belonged to the legs, and it was Lucille Ball, with her trademark red hair coiffed to perfection. Now, that was a star!

Lucy didn't arrive with a big entourage of people, but one underage kid was hanging around the hall who claimed to be with Lucy. He looked like a fan without credentials, so I tried to kick him out of the studio. His name was Michael Stern, and why do I know that? Because he was, as Lucy dubbed him, her "Number One Fan." Well, that fan became Lucy's dear friend and helped make the last years of her life happy not only as her companion but as a pretty good backgammon opponent. (Okay, Michael, now am I forgiven for trying to kick you out?)

Most of the celebrities were kind to the tour groups. For every John Wayne who stopped to say hello to thank his fans, dozens of stars wouldn't even give the tours a wave. Singer/Writer Paul Williams was frequently at NBC in those days. I was on a first-name basis with him, and he was always kind, happily chatting with the people on tour. On one occasion, Pete Hammond brought an old photo of Paul to share with him, so I knocked on Paul's dressing room door. Not only was he delighted to see the picture of himself dressed as a Christmas Nutcracker, he told us the story of the photo. Paul remembered it was from a sketch he'd done years ago on a children's show. He remarked that he was so thin because he'd dieted down to be underweight so he couldn't be drafted into the Vietnam War. He said he was about 110 pounds in the picture.

Another time, an actor approached me in the hallway, pulled me aside, and asked, "Do you think the cue card guy is a dicky-licker?"

Honest to God, I had no idea what he was talking about. By the slight accent in his voice, I imagine this was a homophobic term that had been reserved for whatever part of the South he had once lived.

Stuck between a rock and a redneck, I said, "I don't know. But he seems nice."

Pete would see Garry Shandling around Studio 3 when *Sanford and Son* was being taped. He wasn't happy and told Pete, "I'm quitting Sanford. I'm going to do stand-up full time."

Pete couldn't understand how Garry could give up being Story Editor on one of the network's top shows to be a comic. Pete also remembers having the most incredible stroke of luck on a tour. He hit the comedy goldmine outside a stage when "some of the greatest comedians of time all broke for lunch. They all walked by my tour, and they were all playing it up—Bob Hope, Milton Berle, you name 'em. It was unbelievable. Sometimes, you'd just get lucky like that."

Dinah Brein was responsible for handling the show's phone lines, when who came running down the hallway but John Belushi. He wasn't working in the building; perhaps he was visiting a friend. Somehow, John got wind that Dinah had a diet pill her doctor had prescribed for her. He badgered her and badgered her, even following her to the Page lounge, where she reached for the lone pill in her purse. Dinah told him, "It's not going to get you high. You're just not going to be hungry."

When conducting tours, we were always on the lookout for celebrity sights. Sometimes, celebrities would sneak up behind the tourists. Other times, such as the case with Courtney Conte, Don Rickles just breezed past him and the tourists and said, "Nice zit." Roxanne (Yamaguchi) Moster had a life-saving encounter while giving a tour in the hallway. Roxanne was standing in front of the *Hollywood Squares* set when she felt a sharp pain in her abdomen and passed out. When she came to, *CPO Sharkey* stars Don Rickles and Peter Isacksen were carrying her to the nurse's station. She was able to thank them when she returned to work, following emergency surgery.

The most memorable hallway entrance in my experience was that of stand-up comic and actress Totie Fields. She was a frequent guest on all the talk shows and always delivered her jokes with the rat-a-tat timing of a female Don Rickles. Totie was a loud, funny, round lady who wore beautiful dresses and always had her hair and nails done. Like Rickles, she was beloved. Totie was diabetic and against her doctor's advice had a cosmetic surgical procedure. It resulted in numerous complications, eventually requiring additional surgery, and her left leg had to be amputated above the knee. There were more surgeries, two heart attacks, and a great deal of weight loss. But, you can't keep a good woman down, and in what must have been the crowning moment of her recovery, she agreed to be a star sitting in one of the *Hollywood Squares.*

Hundreds of people were lining the way for Totie to make her entrance. She emerged from her car to thunderous applause that continued as she was wheeled from the midway area to Studio 3. There wasn't a dry eye in the crowd, including Totie. She was overwhelmed by the love and support shown to her. And when the lights came up and host Peter Marshall asked her a question, Totie was back to making people laugh again.

The CBs:

I had risen high enough in the Page ranks (or someone got sick, it could have gone either way) to be assigned the highly coveted assignment of CB. Back in the day, when TV was live and people had to watch it that way, advertisers were given a private room next to the control booth. This allowed advertisers to view the shows they were paying for as they were broadcast. This area was known as the "Client's Booth," now an arcane area, but the Page that would tend to these cigarette pushers and floor wax advertisers became known as the CB.

Two phones per studio were dedicated to the crew and production company members during rehearsal and taping. One was primarily for incoming calls, the other for outgoing. We were to answer the phone, then go into the studio or dressing room to find the person needed. If they weren't available, we were to take a detailed message and put it on the bulletin board next to the daily schedule. We were also encouraged to ask the people making outgoing calls to keep it brief. When the studio was empty, the Pages frequently occupied these phones, taking full advantage of free long-distance phone calls to friends and family around the country.

The CB job gave us a break from tours and ushering and a chance to meet our potential future employers. Tom Hansen was assigned to the 1977 *Bob Hope Christmas Special.* He was called into Eba's office and given the good news. Tom, new to the staff, asked, "Why me?" Eba replied, "Everyone knows you don't want to get into production; you want to get into sales. This way, I will show no favoritism and won't get complaints from the other Pages." Tom remembered the coolest part of the job was going over phone messages with Bob Hope. After all, he said, "I was sitting next to Bob freakin' Hope!"

From his CB position, Tom was the unwitting accomplice of game show warm-up announcer Gene Wood. You'd know Gene's voice from announcing shows like *Password Plus* and the Richard Dawson version of *Family Feud.* Gene was always known for his energetic and sweaty shenanigans, running through the aisles and telling bad jokes before the show was taped and during commercial breaks. If Gene spotted Tom, he'd motion for him to come over and ask him his name. His reply would be, "Tom." Gene would ask again and get the same reply. Then Gene would make a Tom-Tom joke that was slightly racially insensitive and not at all funny, leaving Tom to ponder, "How does this guy have a job?"

On sitcoms, such as *Sanford and Son* and *Chico and the Man*, producers paid union scale a couple of hundred dollars to an audience warm-up guy. This was usually a comic who had the unenviable task of keeping the crowd energetic for hours during a taping. With two audiences, one for the rehearsal and one for the show, that meant 8 – 12 hours of work telling jokes, answering questions, doing magic tricks – anything to entertain the audience. Tom Hansen thought he'd dodged a bullet when he left his job parking cars at the world-renowned Chasen's restaurant only to find himself face-to-face with his least favorite celebrity, Harvey Korman. "People like Dean Martin, Carol Burnett, Jack Benny, they were always nice to the valets, but Korman was an asshole!" Sure enough, Tom was assigned to CB a short-lived comedy series titled (you guessed it), *The Harvey Korman Show*. Tom recalled the audience warm-up guy was doing a funny bit about *Star Trek*. "He was getting a lot of laughs, more laughs than the sitcom, and in the middle of the bit, Korman yelled, 'Get him off, GET HIM OFF!' Korman was a mean guy." The first rule of audience warm-up: Don't upstage The Star!

In the Spring of 1978, a truly special "special" was taped in Studio 4 titled *Ringo*. Another of my bucket list items, to borrow a phrase from the first album I bought, was to Meet The Beatles. The star-studded special was an updated retelling of Mark Twain's *Prince and The Pauper* with Ringo Starr. Having a stressful time coping with fame, he trades places with a hapless nerd who sells Maps to the Star's homes, a fellow named Ognir Rats (Ringo Starr spelled backward). The special was written by two of the hottest variety show writers of that era, Neil Israel and Pat Proft. It was directed by multi-Emmy Award-winning director Jeff Margolis. Ringo sang many of his greatest hits and interacted with a cast that included Carrie Fisher, John Ritter, Angie Dickinson, Vincent Price, and Art Carney. George Harrison narrated, but I never saw George in the studio. This little-known treasure is available on YouTube.

In a serendipitous move of synergy, *The Mike Douglas Show* came from Philadelphia to Burbank to tape for a few weeks on Studio 2, directly across the hall from where Ringo was taping. Ringo used the opportunity to have Mike Douglas interview Ognir Rats, and that footage was used on

Ringo's special. A few minutes later, Mike did a second interview with the real Ringo, who sat down for a chat that ran on *The Mike Douglas Show* to promote his upcoming special.

Ringo was surrounded by his entourage, and always took time to smile and wave to the people who were lining the hallway, falling all over themselves, hoping a little of his Stardust would rub off on them. Being the total show biz professional, I restrained myself from fangirling all over him, even when we made eye contact as he flashed a peace sign. Much like meeting the Pope, given the opportunity, I would have kissed any of his numerous rings.

Lesa Lindsay got the assignment to work the special, answer the phones in the hallway, and direct people to their dressing rooms. She had a Close Encounter of the First Kind with Ringo. Lesa told me she answered the hallway phone, and Ringo's ex-wife was on the line, demanding to speak to him. Lesa went on to say, "She threatened me, screaming, 'I'll have your job.'

I was really scared. I knocked on Ringo's dressing room door and told him his ex-wife was on the phone screaming, and if I didn't get you on the phone, she'd have my job.

Ringo smirked and said, 'Darling, she couldn't do your job.' I was so relieved, and he was so nice.

I went right back to the phone and told her, 'He's busy,' and hung up."

You never know what you're going to get into when you go into the talent's dressing room. We were always instructed to knock on the dressing room door before entering and to announce ourselves. That didn't stop some of the talent from welcoming us into their rooms while they were in various states of undress or in a dress that needed to be zipped up. More than a few times, I'd walk in on a male celebrity sitting in his underwear, waiting to put his pants on just before going to the stage to avoid getting his slacks wrinkled. Once, I saw retired quarterback Joe Namath sitting in what looked like swim trunks, taping his knees before struggling to walk down the hall to his guest appearance on a show.

During taping on Studio 4 of the short-lived variety series, *Van Dyke and Company,* I had one of those you-had-to-be-there-to-believe-it moments. I was working across the hall at Studio 2 when one of the Pages handed me a few phone messages. I looked at the names, but didn't recognize any of them, so I stuffed the pink pieces of paper in my pocket.

A few hours later, I overheard some people talking in the hallway, and one of them called my name. I went over to the man, and he said, "You're not the Shelley Herman I was looking for." A second man smiled and said, "Follow me." He guided me up the stairs into the Control Room of Studio 4, where I met "The Other Shelley Herman," a petite woman with curly hair who was an assistant to the producers of *Van Dyke and Company*. We've remained friends to this day, even at one time sharing the same tax accountant.

The CB was also in charge of the "Tapes and Holds." The Supervisor attached to the show would give the CB a list of seats to save until the last minute before taping began. These seats were usually reserved for the VIPs, some of whom would be waiting outside with the general public, while others were with the talent in the dressing room or arrived shortly before the show began. Often, I would Tape and Hold seats for the talent's friends and family, and I was happy that Steve Martin's parents and I were on a first-name basis. Other celebrities were a little more secretive about their guests, like Orson Welles. We would have to Tape and Hold a seat for a shill he'd have planted in the audience while dazzling Johnny with his magic tricks. On one variety special, the production company had us sign an NDA (Non-Disclosure Agreement) that forbids me to tell anyone a certain magician used twin little people to do his illusion.

More than a few of my fellow Pages have told me stories of knocking on dressing room doors to give celebrities a phone message, only to be greeted by both men and women in various stages of undress or cross-dressed. It's mind-boggling how many women and men needed help with their zippers.

The one CB assignment I wanted the most was to be the Page in charge of the 1976 New Year's Eve *Tonight Show*. For more years than I can remember, I would be babysitting on New Year's Eve, watching *The Tonight Show*, dreaming of someday being part of their party. Now, I was in charge of the show all week! I wanted to think it was because I was the most qualified, but it was the week between Christmas and New Year, and most of the Pages were probably out of town visiting their families.

Actor James Stewart was the first guest that night. I greeted him at his limo in the midway, and his driver asked Mr. Stewart if it would be all right if I took a Polaroid photo of the two of them together. Not only was Mr. Stewart pleased to oblige, he then handed the camera to the limo driver and said, "Take a photo of the little lady and me together." The limo driver gave me the photo, and Mr. Stewart hugged me and wished me a Happy New Year.

That's all I remember from that evening, in large part because of the Polaroid, because several hours later, I was rushed to the hospital. I'd been feeling a bit tired, but chalked it up to just completing finals in college, working long hours, and driving about an hour each way to work and back. I stumbled home and, hours later, called my parents to inform them my neck looked like a bullfrog. My glands were swollen, and I had a 102° fever. I was unable to keep my eyes open. It turns out, SuperPageGirl had a severe case of mononucleosis that turned into hepatitis. When I heard the news, the first thought that crossed my mind was: I hope I didn't just kill James Stewart!

Lesa remembers how kind James Stewart was to her backstage while was working the CB position. "I had to be available to guard the backstage and answer the phones. The night Jimmy Stewart came on, I was standing in the hallway. I was watching Johnny do the monologue on the TV monitor in Jimmy Stewart's dressing room, thinking I was out of sight. I wasn't. Mr. Stewart invited me to sit down and watch it with him! He was such a kind, heartwarming gentleman."

Jim McDonald had the eeriest experience as a CB on January 17, 1977, when he worked on a variety special in which Johnny Cash was a performer. One of the cardinal rules of show biz, the biggest no-no of them all, is to interrupt a TV taping while it is in progress. It can literally cost the production company thousands of dollars if there is downtime, or the talent and union members could go into overtime. So when Jim got a phone call from the Governor of Utah, Scott M. Matheson, he had to make a choice.

Governor Matheson was calling on behalf of Gary Gilmore, a convicted double murderer who was about to be executed by firing squad. It was the top news story of the day, as it was Gilmore's choice to die this way. By doing so, he would become the first to be person executed in nearly a decade, thereby reinstating the death penalty. Gilmore wanted to talk to Johnny Cash, who, as we learned, had been praying with Gilmore while he was incarcerated. Gilmore had two stays of execution, but this was it. He would die this evening.

Jim ran onto Studio 4, waving his hand in the air, yelling to stop the taping at the top of his lungs! Everyone turned to see what the commotion was all about as Jim walked up to Johnny Cash and whispered, "Gary Gilmore wants to talk to you." Cash put down his guitar, went into the hallway and spoke to Gary, uninterrupted for quite some time. He then returned to the studio, the crew resumed their jobs, and the taping continued. At the exact time Gary was being executed, everyone stopped, looked at their watches, and remained silent in prayer and out of respect and consideration for Johnny Cash.

The OICs:

The OIC, Outside in Charge Page, was assigned to wrangle the guests. This assignment came with a clipboard filled with the names of the Groups, VIPs, Regular Ticket Holders, and the Stand-By Guests, some of whom had already been turned away from the show they came to see, so they were understandably a little more high-strung than the others. The job required equal parts courtesy and authority, as the Page with the clipboard was usually a guest's first contact with NBC. As far as gaining entry to the taping, the OIC was the head honcho for the show. Jeff Macker recalled chatting with an audience member at *The Midnight Special* about the margaritas at the Mexican restaurant across the street. A few minutes later the guy returned, Styrofoam cup in hand with Jeff's "coffee" (no salt, on the rocks).

The various groups were in separate lines. This made it stressful when many people, waiting an hour or more in the hot sun, watched a busload of guests pull up to the entrance and go into the studio before them. To ensure an audience for the less popular shows or shows taping at an unusual time, NBC would pay groups of people to stay for the entire taping. These groups would often be from non-profit organizations like churches or PTAs looking for enjoyable fundraising activities to help pay for school supplies. With large groups of a few dozen or more, NBC would pay for the bus to pick them up. Pay was based on the number of people who attended the taping. It was a win-win situation, as long as the attendees didn't fall asleep or get bored and stopped reacting to the sitcom or game show they were watching. I pity the warm-up guy who had to keep these groups entertained for hours in-between the scenes.

Another activity that took place in line was what some male Pages described to me as "Pulling Tail." Other male Pages would find lovely young female tourists who were only in town a few days and make the slick moves on them, pulling them out of the General Admission line, and slipping them into the VIP section. That would usually lead to drinks, dinner and, in one case, a short-lived marriage.

Now, this can be done harmlessly, as was the case with Sandy (Crompton) Selma. She was a school teacher with no aspirations to be in the entertainment industry. She was given VIP tickets to see *The Tonight Show* from a dear family friend, Stanley Robertson, NBC's first Black vice president. By her admission, she said she was a little too dressed up for a TV show taping, but that's Sandy. To this day, she is always totally put together, sewing her own clothes, and she was the first girl I knew who did silk wraps on her long, elegant fingernails.

Soon the male Pages working *The Tonight Show* line were circling her like a school of sharks. Sandy was not only a beautiful, intelligent Black woman; she knew Stanley Robertson! Three Black male Pages started talking to Sandy and asked her, "Would you like to be an NBC Page?" Sandy had no idea what a Page was, but these young men assured her they'd be right there by her side to shepherd her through the process. Sandy told me, "They were pitching the Page job. They were so engrossed in me becoming a Page, so they set up an appointment the next Monday morning with Eba Hawkins right there on the spot." Page Supervisor

Frank Grant asked her if she could be there at 10:00 a.m. for the interview, then slipped Sandy a copy of the Page manual to take home and study before Monday's all-important meeting. Of course, Sandy got the job but she had to give her two weeks' notice to the school before she could begin. With her background as a teacher, Eba hired Sandy specifically to help with the children's tours.

I have a distinct memory of being the OIC on a hot summer day. For months, I had been hounding the NBC nurse, telling her that we should teach the Pages this new thing the Red Cross was touting: CPR or Cardiopulmonary Resuscitation. Daily, we'd deal with thousands of visitors taking tours and seeing shows, but none of us were prepared in case of a medical emergency. Tim Danker and I volunteered to be the first two Pages to complete the course, and sure enough, that same afternoon, a man passed out in line at *The Tonight Show*! It all happened so quickly, but I remember it all in slow motion. I heard the commotion, then someone screamed, so I flung the all-important clipboard to the ground, took off my blazer, and ran to the man's aid.

When I reached the guest, his eyes were open, but he was red in the face, sweating, and a bit disoriented. I kept repeating the instructions I'd learned in my head, "Look, listen, and feel." I wadded up my blazer and placed it under his head. His wife, still upset, leaned down to me and said, "Our son is a paramedic. You're doing a nice job." I turned to the man and said, "Go ahead and pass out again. I just got my CPR certificate, and I could use the practice!" We all laughed, and that eased the tension. Someone called an ambulance, which took my patient and his wife a few blocks away to St. Joseph's Hospital. I gave them my name and asked them to call me to let me know everything was okay. I also promised to provide them with a VIP ticket to *The Tonight Show* whenever they returned.

Well, my patient survived, but I never did see him again. A few weeks later, an enormous box addressed to me arrived in the Page lounge. It was from my patient, who, it turns out, was an executive with the 3M tape company. Not only did I receive a lovely thank you note, but the box also contained every kind of tape a girl could ever hope to have: a variety of office tape, clear and brown packing tape, VHS and Beta tapes, tape with Christmas decorations, even pink tape to make pin curls in my hair! It was overwhelmingly hysterical, and I was grateful for the gift.

The DFs:

There was one more class of guests that you'll never hear about or see written about because, officially, they don't exist. These were and still are The DFs, The Down Fronts. Pages were required to discreetly pull men and women under the age of twenty-five who were attractive and well-dressed, to sit in the first few rows at the taping. Johnny never wanted to see people in the audience with gray hair while he did the monologue. He wanted a young, enthusiastic crowd looking back at him. Jay Leno even upped the ante on the youth market when he hosted *The Tonight Show,* as he came running onto stage to the thunderous applause and high-fives of his eager, young, good-looking fans. We had to carefully chat up the guests to ensure they weren't just holding a place on the line for their granny or crazy uncle. We'd ask them to follow us and direct them to a line with other beautiful people just out of sight of the general public. I know, it was sexist, ageist, and a perfect opportunity for the male Pages to "Pull Tail." I was not too fond of the rules, but I had to play by them.

Chapter Four

DID SOMEBODY CALL A LIMO?

One of the most sought-after assignments was the Limo Runs. A Page would be given the task of escorting a star to any number of activities, such as a press event or personal appearance. The stars were usually traveling alone as it was on NBC's nickel. Often, we would pick them up at the airport, or escort them from their home or hotel, to make sure the talent would meet their plane before take-off. They were usually alone, with no family, publicists, or managers. So, it became incumbent on us to deliver the star to their destination, come hell or high water.

This job was the ultimate field trip, a welcome break from touring the hallways. But it was always a challenge to me, as I tend to get slightly motion sick. If the talent lived in the hills, I made sure always to take a Dramamine, or have mints in my purse. It was up to the talent to decide if the Page would sit with them in the back seat of the limo, or ride shotgun in the front next to the driver.

Many stars were gracious enough to allow us into their homes to wait while they collected their luggage and bid their families goodbye. Conrad Bain, Mr. Drummond on *Diff'rent Strokes*, was incredibly kind, offering me some water as he saw that I looked a little wonky. I clearly remember Gil Gerard, star of *Buck Rogers in the 25th Century*, calling his family from the newly installed space-age communicator in the limo: a mobile car phone! Lee Remick and Larry Linville come to mind as engaging as we drove to the airport. One sitcom co-star asked if we could stop by "Jack's house" on Mulholland Drive to get some cocaine for the ride to the airport. I politely said if he did, he'd miss his plane. Some wanted me to join them on the plane to continue my job after hours as they jetted out to some personal appearance. Who knew my itchy little polyester uniform could be so arousing?

It seems women weren't the only objects of desire on limo runs. Jeff Garrett had a world-renowned male director invite him to sit in the back of the limousine. They struck up a friendly conversation, and soon The Director was massaging Jeff's hand, admiring his ring. Jeff felt uneasy, and it became apparent The Director wanted more than a limo ride. He wanted to ride Jeff!

Jeff also had a limo run with LaWanda Page, best remembered as Aunt Esther from the *Sanford and Son* series. Jeff was taken by limo to her home in South Los Angeles and escorted her to an event. At the time, it was a rundown part of town. Jeff went to her apartment, and as she opened the door, she exclaimed, "Do me!" For a moment, Jeff was speechless. He couldn't help but notice the numerous photos on the walls of LaWanda's apartment from when she was an exotic dancer. The images featured her wearing nothing more than pasties.

She demanded again, 'Honey, do me," and she turned her back to Jeff to reveal that she needed to be zipped into her dress. She'd just done her nails and couldn't do it herself. Crisis averted. Once they were settled into the limo, she whipped out a joint and asked Jeff to do her again. It's a good thing we always had Bic lighters in our pockets. The people who wrote the Page manual could never have imagined this scenario.

Tommy Patino was given the limo run to pick up *Chico and the Man* co-star Della Reese from her home. Tommy was surprised to see she had an indoor pool in her living room. Tom told me he thought, "Wow, these rich people know how to live!"

Renee Palyo and I flipped a coin, and she won the dream-of-a-lifetime opportunity. She got to pick up Fred Astaire and bring him to the Century Plaza, a glamorous hotel near Beverly Hills, for a press conference to promote his TV movie, *A Family Upside Down*. Having read David Niven's book about Fred Astaire, Renee was primed for the ride.

In their twenty-minute limo ride, Renee mentioned, "I read a lot about you from David Niven."

Astaire replied, "Oh, David made up a lot of those stories."

Renee remembers Astaire was frail, and thin. He'd been retired from acting up until this last movie. He said to Renee, "People would ask me how I came up with all those routines. I said I just danced."

Renee took him into the ballroom to meet the awaiting press. She recalled he didn't do very well, but in the end, Renee went on to say, "People came up with memorabilia. It was all very nice."

When we got to the limo, he asked, 'How did I do?'

I said, 'You were fabulous.' As he was getting into the limo, he kissed me on the cheek. It is a lovely memory."

Pete Hammond met Sally Field in Malibu and took her to the airport to promote the TV movie mini-series *Sybil*. She didn't want to be driven to Malibu on the return trip. Instead, she asked the limo to take her to a house on Miller Drive. There, Pete saw a fake Oscar trophy inscribed that read, "To the Greatest Ass in Hollywood." The limo had taken them to Burt Reynold's home. I guess he liked her. He really liked her! Or had she given him the award?

Sue Walsh, a sweet, soft-spoken Page who looked like model Cheryl Tiegs, was given comic Richard Pryor for the day. Richard, who wasn't often easily pleased, reciprocated Sue's kindness by sending her a gold cigarette case engraved, "To Sue, Thanks, Richard."

Years later, Sue's husband, producer Paul Brownstein joined Richard and his wife, Jennifer, as they limoed to a comedy awards event. Paul whipped out the gold cigarette case and asked if Richard remembered Sue. Richard answered, "Yeah. I fucked her." For the record, no, he didn't, but Richard did get a big laugh from Paul.

Dinah Brein had what she thought would be a simple limo run to the home of *Wheel of Fortune* host Chuck Woolery. As the limo pulled up to the front door, Dinah saw Chuck's then-wife, actress JoAnn Pflug, throwing a lot of Chuck's belongings onto the front yard. Dinah asked the limo driver if they were at the right house, and he replied, "That's what it says." Soon, the back door of the limo opened, and a flustered Chuck told the driver to "Step on it!" Then Chuck looked to Dinah and said, "Let's just forget this ever happened."

Even more startling than that encounter, Courtney Conte told me he had the limo run from hell. He was stuck escorting, in his words, "The most anti-Semitic guy on the planet, Ned Beatty, who was spewing anti-Semitic references" while on their ride.

Every New Year's Day, NBC telecast the *Tournament of Roses* parade live from Pasadena, California. I worked on the broadcast for three years, and it was always freakishly cold. We weren't allowed to wear coats over our uniforms, and heaven forbid we wore tights to fend off the damp sunrise chill. I was fortunate to spend some of the mornings in the heated, clear geodesic dome occupied by parade hosts Michael Landon and local news personality Kelly Lange, getting them coffee, snacks, and anything else I could think of to get out of the cold.

Pete Hammond lived about an hour from the studio and chose to sleep in the Page lounge one New Year's Eve to catch some extra z's. He arranged for the limo to pick him up at work before meeting the NBC star he took to the parade. At 4:00 a.m. New Year's Day, other Pages were taken, by limo, to escort the talent from their homes (or wherever they were) to the staging area of the parade route an hour before the telecast began. This call time could prove challenging.

Some stars were camera-ready, hair and makeup in place, while others weren't and needed a quick visit to the makeup trailers. More than a few stars miscalculated and stayed awake all New Year's Eve partying. The results had the Pages handing out hot coffee, aspirin, or whatever beverage was required. In one case, they had to clean up a certain heartthrob, who vomited all over his clothes in the limo before his arrival.

Tommy Patino was assigned to make sure Jim Hutton and David Wayne, stars of the NBC series *Ellery Queen*, made it to the Rose Parade on time. When the limo retrieved them on New Year's Eve, it was apparent they'd been partying all night long. They were still pretty buzzed when they arrived in Pasadena. Then, to Tommy's horror, Jim Hutton asked the limo driver to open the sunroof.

Jim and David jumped up and stuck their heads through the roof while barreling down Fair Oaks Blvd. The crisp, fresh morning air did nothing to sober them up as they waved to the crowds on the parade route, all the while Jim was screaming, "I'm Ellery Queen! This is my dad!"

When the parade concluded, a lucky few Pages were assigned to work at the Rose Bowl Stadium and could watch the football game live or in the hospitality tent, NBC provided to its VIPs. The hospitality suites were always lavish, with more food or booze than could possibly be consumed in an afternoon.

Jeff Garrett had the easiest job, or at least he thought he did. Jeff was assigned to sit at a table and make sure no one else sat there, as it was reserved for the President of the network. Then Zsa Zsa Gabor showed up. At this stage of her career, she was probably best known for appearing on game shows like *Hollywood Squares*, as she had become more of a TV personality than an actor. Zsa Zsa had a carefully cultivated image of a woman who had divorced well. She would pepper her conversations with one-liners like, *"I am a marvelous housekeeper. Every time I leave a man, I keep his house"* Oh, and she was arrested (and served time in jail) for slapping a Beverly Hills police officer when he stopped the actress for driving her Rolls Royce with expired registration tags.

Her haute couture persona made her rather haughty and, frankly, not nice. Zsa Zsa became insistent that she be allowed to sit at the empty table Jeff had been entrusted to protect. Jeff, sensing his job was on the line over this bourgeois bitch, finally had to tell her in no uncertain terms, "If you sit down, I'll have to haul your ass out of this tent!"

Lucie Arnaz overheard the kerfuffle and said to Jeff, in front of Zsa Zsa, "Good job!"

Zsa Zsa told them both to "Fuck off," then turned on her designer heels and left the suite.

Some Pages got more eclectic assignments. One of these "get out of tour jail" gigs went to Al Ovadia, who found himself running up and down the manicured greens in his Page uniform, shagging balls at Bob Hope's personal home golf course. It was a clever idea that allowed the press an opportunity to interview and photograph Bob in his natural habitat.

During one of the press tours, I was assigned to the hospitality suite at The Century Plaza Hotel. I scored one of the cushiest jobs a Page could ever hope to have. Five days in the Presidential Suite! NBC let me stay overnight, which worked out well, as I could stand on the balcony each evening and watch the sunset over the Pacific Ocean. The hotel would dry clean my uniform every night and have it ready for me when I woke up, and, the biggest perk of all, I could order anything off the room service menu for free!

My job was to open the suite at 8:00 a.m. and ensure the hotel provided food and beverages throughout the day. I also learned how to send the "copy" the journalists had written to their news organizations throughout the day. For example, Richard Hack trained me to use his Exxon Qwip, a silver cylindrical device that transmitted his daily reports at the lightning speed of six-minutes pages per minute to his editors at The Hollywood Reporter. All day long, I'd watch the machines around the suite spin, and voilà, the words got wherever there were supposed to be, ready for the newspaper and magazine editors around the world to do their thing. Occasionally, a celebrity would come by the suite to have an adult beverage or to have their hair and makeup touched up. It was quite the parade of talent!

After living among the stars on the 19th floor, on the fourth day, I became a bit weary. I couldn't lock up the suite until after 1:00 a.m. as the press wanted to hang around to talk and drink, and drink, and drink. Even in this rarefied environment, I was getting burnt out eating steaks for every meal. On the last day, I had room service bring me a peanut butter and jelly sandwich along with a Diet Coke. You can take the Page out of Burbank, but you can't take the Burbank out of the Page.

Before the new season of shows began airing in September, the NBC Guest Relations Department and the Press and Publicity Departments gathered all their network stars to meet with representatives from the press. Entertainment reporters traveled from around the country to get their touch-of-greatness moments with current and new network stars. These reports would air shortly before the season premieres of the fall shows in the local news, and in the markets that carried NBC programs. The network types glad-handed all the stars. There was the promise of hit shows in the air. And there were tons of free food and adult beverages!

In the years I was with NBC, these events were held on a Saturday and Sunday at The Sheraton Universal Hotel, the venue often used by out-of-town guests who appeared on *The Tonight Show.* Johnny would refer to the hotel as the "Sheraton Unbearable."

It was a perfect site to have Pages escort the talent from one poolside hotel room to the next. Every room was personalized with banners to identify the city each entertainment reporter represented. A Page was assigned to accompany a series star for the day. Each interview had to be a tight 15 minutes, as the talent had to move on to the next reporter, then the next reporter, who would all pretty much ask the same questions like "Tell us about your character" or "Did you do your own stunts?"

The fast-paced day didn't stop the stars from hitting on everyone: the Pages, the throngs of fans who caught wind they were in the building – or, in one case, the daughter of an NBC affiliate owner. Thankfully, I wasn't the Page who had to pull a particular blond actor off an underage girl and get him back to his round of interviews.

On rare occasions, the press would gather in the hotel's ballroom to interview a big star, like Fred Astaire, when he was promoting his TV movie. I had been assigned to walk quickly up and down the aisle with a microphone so the press could ask questions of Mr. Astaire. I was so afraid I'd be clumsy and trip in front of one of the most incredible dancers who ever lived. It was one long, sweaty hour for me, but when the Q&A session finally ended, I was overwhelmed because Mr. Astaire told me how "gracefully" I'd handled myself. (Swoon!)

Tom Chasuk had a slightly different experience when he escorted an actress, a big sex symbol at the time, who seemed a little tipsy. She liked her coffee prepared a particular way...with a generous pour of Jack Daniel's. Just as a reporter was about to roll tape to begin an interview, she asked to take a moment to get a cup of coffee. The reporter jumped to his feet to pour her coffee from the fresh pot in his suite. She caught Tommy's eye and said demurely, "Oh no, that won't be necessary. Tom knows what I like in my coffee."

Dinah Brein escorted an enormous barrel-chested star around for the afternoon. As the day progressed, she found it necessary to have the bartender water down his never-ending requests for Bloody Marys. His reputation as a blustering jerk was cemented when he yelled at her that the drink didn't have any vodka in it. Dinah replied, "You've been drinking them like this all afternoon."

My first limo run wasn't very long. I picked up one of the newest stars in the NBC lineup, Erik Estrada, from his modest apartment in Studio City. He was dressed in a nice shirt and the requisite tight jeans of the day, but when the NBC brass spotted him before we entered the press area, they demanded he change into his *ChiPs* uniform. Erik's appearance was to be the first look reporters would get of his character, Officer Frank Poncherello. It was an odd request, but I guess the network felt it was a necessary suggestion. Erik said it would be like having William Shatner show up in his Captain Kirk attire from *Star Trek*. Erik had the understanding the press was there to interview the actor, not the character. But optics are everything, and NBC wasn't about to tolerate Erik's outburst. Erik's co-star, Larry Wilcox, who played Officer Jon Baker in the series, had no problem cooperating with the NBC brass and gladly put on his police uniform to meet the press. Erik was told Larry could do the numerous interviews by himself. Eventually, Erik acquiesced to NBC's demand.

As we rode the escalator to the poolside cabanas, fans were already shouting Erik and Larry's names, begging for autographs. Erik flashed his megawatt smile, and all signs of the previous tension were gone. The press loved them, and two stars were born!

A few months later, a photo of me escorting Erik Estrada at this event appeared in a teen magazine. I was labeled as one of Erik's "Favorite Dates." Years later, I would work for Erik's manager, Helen Azevedo, at their production company based out of Orion Television. Erik didn't remember me. So much for being one of his favorites.

Chapter Five

DRIVING MISS GILDA

If one story deserved to be in the Page Hall of Fame, it would be this one. It took place in June 1977. Pete Hammond and Brian Robinette got the plum assignments to travel via limousine to Los Angeles International Airport to greet two *Saturday Night Live* stars, Gilda Radner and John Belushi. They were entrusted to bring them to The Sheraton Universal Hotel for the annual NBC Affiliates event, a day filled with dozens of interviews with the stations that ran NBC programs. Belushi was a no-show at the last minute, so Brian told me he had the less-than-desirable task of escorting his replacement, "a kind of snide and weird Chevy Chase."

Gilda was America's sweetheart, undoubtedly the breakout female star of *Saturday Night Live*. She'd worked for years doing improvisational comedy shows and came to *SNL* fully equipped with characters and catchphrases. They included: hard-of-hearing senior citizen Emily Litella (Nevermind...), and another Weekend Update character, the caustic Roseanne Roseannadanna (It's always something.) Gilda also played the ultimate nerd-girl Lisa Loopner (That's so funny I forgot to laugh), and my favorite, Judy Miller (Nothing, mom), the young girl wearing her Brownie uniform with a half-slip on her head that was meant to resemble lush, flowing hair. Not even news icon Barbara Walters was safe from being lovingly impersonated when Gilda, speech impediment and all, played Baba Wawa. Working alongside Jane Curtin and Laraine Newman, Gilda became the only female Not Ready for Prime Time Player to win an Outstanding Performance Emmy Award for her work on the show. She was funny and fearless. Gilda also had a sweetness and fragility that made every girl want to be her and every guy wanted to take care of her.

After Pete escorted Gilda through the gauntlet of NBC affiliates, she was invited to dinner by another network star, Bill Bixby, and his wife, Brenda Benet. She politely declined, then turned to Pete and said, "Grab a couple of your friends. I've never been to Los Angeles before, and I have a couple of hours before I have to fly back. Take me on a tour of the city!"

Pete asked two other Pages working the event, Linda Levinson and Melissa Hunt, to join them as they took off in Pete's white 1976 Mustang. They drove through the canyon, over the hill to Westwood, where they dined on falafels and Stan's Donuts. Linda shared with me the following entries from her journal:

"Why don't you pull over at that market, Pete," Gilda said as she took her first bite of the hot donut. "I can run in and buy a box of sugar and just pour it down my throat." Pete continued, "Gilda loved the donut, but wanted to let us know it was a little bit sweet for her taste. We thought she was hysterical and laughed long and hard. She tossed the rest of the donuts and jammed a mouthful of bubble gum into her mouth."

The adventure continued as the trio headed to Hollywood. Pete continued the story, "It was dusk as we drove up to Sunset Boulevard to Grauman's Chinese Theatre. We were like children in front of the famous theatre with all the hands and footprints in the cement. Gilda tried fitting into the tiniest little high heel prints and the biggest cowboy (boot) indentations. More laughs, lots of tourists, and no one recognized Gilda."

Linda shared some girl talk with Gilda, who gave her advice and encouragement. "Gilda talked about being in her thirties, and how she had been anonymous for a long time. She'd worked in clubs and with ensemble groups perfecting her timing and talent. She talked about being fat, and how hard it was to resist food and keep thin. She talked to us and asked us questions about our lives and our interests. She seemed like someone I wanted to spend a lot of time with, possibly a new and treasured friend. Linda wanted to be a comedy writer, and Gilda said, "Stick with comedy. Look at me. I'm just making it now.""

"After Grauman's, we drove her into the Fairfax area to meet her boyfriend's family. She had the address on a crumpled-up piece of paper.

We didn't have a map, so we drove around in circles for a while until we found our destination. Gilda went in, and we waited in the car. After ten minutes, she was back in the car."

Pete began to get concerned as the needle on his Mustang's fuel gauge was moving uncomfortably close to the letter E. Linda and Gilda, totally unaware of the gas shortage, continued gabbing like girls. Like Cinderella, time was running out for Gilda's enchanted tour of the town.

As Pete rounded the corner of Fairfax and Beverly Boulevards, his car ran out of gas. As hard as he tried, he couldn't start it again. So, what did the able-bodied Pete do? He had Melissa, Linda, and Gilda push the car while he steered it to the gas station a short block away. Pete told me, "It wasn't a big journey. The Texaco gas station was right there. It was kismet." Still, Pete couldn't help but comment on the irony: the car had stopped right in front of CBS, our network rival. So, under the watchful eye of the CBS logo, Pete gassed up the Mustang and drove to a designated location where they met Gilda's limo. Pete parked his car, got into the limo with Gilda, and raced to Los Angeles International Airport, where she made her flight on time.

Pete thought that would be the last contact he had with Gilda, but a few months later, he was surprised to receive the following: a handwritten note on a piece of seagull-themed stationery. It was from Gilda.

"August 21

Dear Pete,

O.K.... I'm a creep...it took me longer than it should of [sic] to write and say thanks for taking care of me. you made my eight hour stay in California into a two month "tourist-delight-package" from "falafels" to "Belairs" My mom always told me you're supposed to write thank-you notes immediately while the nice feelings you have are still on the top of your brain – but a month later – those feels are still there – and I thank you I intended to write right across this bird instead of around him.

I slept the whole way on the plane after I ate everything they gave me and went home and slept a couple of days – happy to at last have mysterious jet-lag – often spoke of as an excuse around the office.

Anyway, as far as Pages are concerned, I figure I had the absolute best one assigned to me – and if life brings me back to L.A. once again – put gas in the car and meet me at the airport!

Thanks again, Pete – say hello to everyone for me – and I still have donut crumbs on my blue pants."

Pete did see Gilda again and warmly greeted her the following year when he was working on the *Emmy Awards* telecast. Pete said, "She was great. She seemed to feel much more comfortable as a star at that point."

Following her divorce from *SNL* musician GE Smith, Gilda married an actor she met while starring in the 1982 film *Hanky Panky*, Gene Wilder. In 1986, Gilda was diagnosed with ovarian cancer, and underwent chemotherapy and radiotherapy treatment until it went into remission. With renewed optimism, she penned a book titled *It's Always Something* detailing her cancer ordeal. On May 17, 1989, while undergoing a CAT scan, Gilda fell into a coma. Three days later, she passed away with her husband by her side. She was only 42. The marker on her grave, located in Stamford, Connecticut, reads, "GILDA RADNER WILDER, Comedienne-Ballerina, 1946 ···1989."

In 1990, Radner was given a posthumous Grammy Award for Best Spoken Word or Non-Musical Recording. Her legacy now includes the Gilda Radner Familial Ovarian Cancer Registry, which helps women and girls with a family history of ovarian cancer. There's also Gilda's Club, part of the Cancer Support Community, which provides emotional support to cancer patients and their families.

As an original SNL cast member, Gilda's legacy as a comedy icon has long been revered by generations of women who followed in her footsteps. On June 27, 2003, 14 years after her passing, Gilda was honored again. Laraine Newman joined fellow *SNL* alumna Molly Shannon, comedy greats The Smothers Brothers, and numerous family and friends when Gilda received a posthumous star on The Hollywood Walk of Fame on the sidewalk where Pete, Linda, and Melissa first showed her the stars that magical evening in 1976.

"I wanted a perfect ending. Now I've learned, the hard way, that some poems don't rhyme, and some stories don't have a clear beginning, middle, and end. Life is about not knowing, having to change, taking the moment, and making the best of it, without knowing what's going to happen next.

Delicious ambiguity. ... Gilda Radner"

Chapter Six

ANDY KAUFMAN -

January 17, 1949 – ?

Andy was already a misunderstood performance artist when I met him at Studio 4, where he made several appearances on the short-lived variety series *Van Dyke and Company*. On the first episode of *Saturday Night Live*, October 11, 1975, Andy's Foreign Man, a precursor to Sasha Baron Cohen's character, Borat, made him an overnight sensation. He also performed a hysterically bizarre routine, lip-syncing to the Mighty Mouse theme song. Andy was invited back to do other bits that involved playing the bongos, singing "Pop Goes the Weasel," and unleashing his signature closer, where he transformed into a spot-on impression of Elvis Presley. Even the real Elvis Presley gave it his approval, saying Andy was the best.

Andy wasn't very social, but he was kind. Andy wouldn't hurt a fly or even a cockroach because he called me one night and asked me to come over to his place to get one out of his bathtub! He also called me a few times when I still lived at home with my parents. My mother would get all excited to hear that Andy Kaufman, a single man with a Jewish surname, was on the other end of the line. Then, I showed mom one of his performances on *Saturday Night Live*, and she immediately backed off.

When he spoke to me, and I looked into those bluer-than-blue eyes, I felt a friendship connection. We'd meet for lunches in NBC's infamous commissary, The Hungry Peacock, where he'd tell me how he was working at a deli to see what it was actually like to work at a restaurant. He was looking to be as authentic with his performances as possible. He would also run ideas by me, and one day at lunch he asked me to help him work on something. Actually, he wanted me to join him on stage at The Improv on Melrose Avenue. I was flattered, and also confused, but I went for it anyway.

So, here was the bit: Andy went on stage and told the audience that show biz wasn't steady work, and he needed something to fall back on. He told them he was attending beauty school by day in the hopes of getting his license to cut hair. There were a few titters of laughter, but most of the crowd was buying it because that was Andy's superpower. Andy could get you to believe the most illogical premises. He then asked for a volunteer to step up from the audience, offering to give them a free haircut so he could practice his newly learned skills. Some hands went up, but it didn't matter because I had been pre-selected. I walked on stage, acting a little scared, which was part of the act. I was genuinely nervous, though, it wasn't a big stretch. Andy proceeded to put a cape around my neck and style my "hair," which was actually a wig. As he spoke, Andy would become increasingly agitated, whacking away at my long wig until someone from the audience jumped to his feet and told him to stop. That only made Andy more upset. I faked a few tears and ran off the stage while Andy argued with the well-meaning man, who was also a shill in the audience. I can't remember if it was Andy's longtime collaborator Bob Zmuda or not, but he was good. When his time on stage was over, Andy was euphoric! The bit worked! He asked me to do it again in a few weeks, but I said no. I didn't get it. It wasn't funny. It was kind of cruel. And we went on after midnight, and I didn't get paid, and I had to go to work and college and didn't have the energy to do it all. And, and, and!

What I didn't realize at the time was this was the germ of an idea that would eventually blossom into Andy's wrestling routine. Andy would go on to become the self-proclaimed "Inter-Gender Wrestling Champion of the World." He'd go on to pick fights with men and women, even the cast of the late-night comedy show, *Fridays*. The actors in all these scenarios were on a need-to-know basis only.

Andy and I kept in touch, and we'd visit each other when he made guest appearances on other shows like *The Midnight Special*. Oddly, he once mentioned that he'd just been hired to star on a new ABC sitcom, but I shouldn't watch it because it was "not very good." That show was *Taxi*, where his Foreign Man got a name: Latka Gravas.

He even caused mischief on the set of *Taxi*. Andy asked for the week off. The producers consented, and on Monday, the cast was told the guest star for the week "may" look familiar, but at no time were they to call him anything other than Tony. Andy arrived on Stage 23 in full make-up, dressed like a completely different person, to play Louie DePalma's brother. Not only that, he arrived with two scantily-clad ladies and caused such an uproar that the security guards at Paramount Studios had to escort him (and his escorts) off the lot. That was Andy's idea of fun!

How do I know all of this? Because my husband, Randall Carver, was there! He played John Burns in the first season of *Taxi,* and he thought Andy's antics were funny—but they weren't so funny for the other series stars like Judd Hirsch and Jeff Conway, who were visibly upset. Tony Danza had his home movie camera rolling when the outburst began but has not been able to locate that precious tape. I would love to have seen it. And, for the record, I went against Andy's advice. I did watch *Taxi* and loved it.

Andy was a health food fanatic. He even got me to eat raw cashews as a snack, which were horrible and tasted like paste-but I wanted to get along, so I ate along. He did, however, love to eat lots of chocolate cake and other sweets in the commissary. I never saw Andy drink alcohol, smoke weed, or smoke cigarettes, but I did see his character, Tony Clifton, with a cigarette in hand. Again, the man was a mass of contradictions. That's why news of his rare large-cell carcinoma lung cancer diagnosis was met with skepticism. Andy had bragged that someday, he would fake his death, then return years later. But it wasn't an elaborate scheme. Andy died May 16, 1984, in Los Angeles at age thirty-five.

Sixteen years after his death, Andy did come back in the form of Jim Carrey, whose uncanny performance of Latka Gravas in the movie *Man on the Moon* even mesmerized the original *Taxi* cast members who worked alongside him in the film. Fun fact, Jim and Andy share the same birthday, January 17. Some people still don't think that's a coincidence.

Chapter Seven

MY LUCY RICARDO THINKING CAP

Once I had my Page uniform and access to all the buildings on the lot, I set my sights on meeting Dick Ebersol. Dick had been named Vice President of Late Night Programming at NBC. Dick held the distinction of being the first Vice President at NBC under the age of 30. For ten years, reruns of *The Tonight Show* aired on Saturdays in the talk show's usual late-night time slot. But when Johnny renegotiated his contract, he no longer wanted those episodes to air on Saturday. Instead, he'd use them during the week, allowing Johnny more vacation days and fewer guest hosts. To fill the newly vacant slot, Dick met with Lorne Michaels to discuss the development of a new late-night series, *NBC's Saturday Night Live*. It's safe to say late-night television has never been the same since *Saturday Night Live* premiered with guest host George Carlin on October 11, 1975.

While the series was "Live from New York," Dick had an office in Burbank where he met his wife, *Wheel of Fortune* co-host Susan Stafford. After knowing each other for eighteen days, they were in love. Susan (who is devoutly religious) and Dick were married on the beach, in front of the home of *The Midnight Special* Producer Burt Sugarman, and his then-wife Carol Wayne (the beautiful blonde best remembered as The Tea Time Lady on *The Tonight Show*). After the minister, Ken Gullickson (the same clergyman who would officiate the wedding of Kris and Robert Kardashian), pronounced them husband and wife, Chevy Chase picked Susan up, bridal dress and all, and threw her into the Pacific Ocean. These sounded like my kind of people. I had to meet them!

I tried to do things by the book and get an appointment to meet Dick when he was in town, but I could never get past his gatekeepers. I wrote letters and even waved to him if I saw him in the hallway. But nothing, no luck. The shortest distance for me hasn't always been a straight line. It would take some out-of-the-box thinking to reach my goal. And who thought better out of the box than Lucy Ricardo on *I Love Lucy*? What is it they say about luck? It's when talent and opportunity meet. So I knew that I had to act boldly and quickly when my opportunity arrived. But what to do? What to do?

Within a few weeks, the moment was right. I was driving home down the 101 Freeway late one evening when I turned on 790 KABC TalkRadio and heard, "My next guest is...Dick Ebersol!" I headed straight for the nearest off-ramp, found a payphone at a well-lit gas station, grabbed a fistful of quarters from the bottom of my purse, and called the show. The call screener picked up the line and asked me what question I had for Dick. So I lied and said it was about something on *Saturday Night Live.* In less than a minute, the talk show host said, "Caller, you're on the air. What's your question?"

I was shaking. I took a deep breath and said, "Hi, Dick. I'm Shelley Herman, and I'm a member of the NBC Page Staff in Burbank. I've been trying for weeks to get an appointment to meet you, but your assistant won't schedule a time." Dick was very cordial and said something nice about the Page staff. I then barreled through, adding, "Can I get a promise from you that when I call your assistant tomorrow, she'll add me to your calendar?"

Dick laughed and said, "Of course," and commended me on my initiative.

Sure enough, I had my meeting with Dick. He asked me about my goals and where I saw myself in five years. I told him I planned on working side-by-side with him and that after he got promoted to President of the network, then finally retired, I would gladly take over the reins to continue his vision. He seemed amused. I asked what advice he could give me, and what he said startled me. Dick's advice was that I should leave NBC.

What? I just got there! He said I should learn what I could at NBC and then leave, because they would value me more with outside experience rather than being promoted from within the company.

It would be a few more years before I left NBC, but I did get another meeting scheduled to see Dick and my ol' pal Andy Kaufman. I was on vacation in New York, and first and foremost, I wanted a tour of 30 Rockefeller Center. Second, I wanted to see *Saturday Night Live*-live. My timing could not have been worse. It was in 1982, and viewers overwhelmingly voted 195,544 times to keep Andy off SNL forever. When I called Dick Ebersol's office to let him know I'd arrived, his assistant told me, "Now is not a good time."

Next, I called George Shapiro, Andy's manager, and the nicest guy in the world, to see if Andy was okay. Yes, Andy was okay. *SNL's* loss was Andy's gain. Ever the performance artist, Andy took the lemons and made lemonade, so there was no time for socializing.

The writing staff was feverishly rewriting behind closed doors. I said a few quick hellos to Andy and Dick during the rehearsal, then got the heck out there, as the whole vibe was extremely intense. Andy had created yet another show biz moment, one for the history books. The ban didn't last forever, and Andy was welcomed back for what would be his last appearance on the show on January 22, 1983.

It wasn't long before Susan and Dick agreed to separate as good friends. Dick was often away, and the two lived platonically under the same roof on San Ysidro Drive in Beverly Hills. Susan walked me through the house, looking for Dick when we stumbled into his bedroom and found him sleeping on his side, wearing only his birthday suit. I tried to act sophisticated and nonchalant, but on the inside, I was a more than a bit flustered. I don't think Susan saw me turn beet red from the shock. She didn't want to disturb him, so we tip-toed to the table for dinner.

Always gracious, Susan was hosting a dinner party that evening with a few close friends. She invited me to be the dinner partner of her dear friend, Father Terry Sweeney, a Jesuit Priest and prolific writer. A few years later, he served as a Technical Consultant on *The Thorn Birds* mini-series starring Richard Chamberlain. Father Sweeney had the deepest blue eyes and was the most handsome dinner dates I never dated.

From the moment I met her, and to this day, Susan Stafford has always been a kind, giving woman-and a lot of fun. The *Wheel of Fortune* fans who came to see her turn the letters (pre-Vanna White) appreciated her naturally warm, affable personality. During commercial breaks, she'd answer questions from the audience. One day, Chevy Chase surprised her and did a pratfall down the bleacher stairs of the audience.

Susan was a gal who couldn't say no when it came to helping others. I remember she once agreed to participate in a fundraiser that required her to run a marathon. Having no experience in long-distance running, Susan chose to train the day before the event. She walked from her home in Beverly Hills to Burbank, about 11.5 miles, down Sunset Blvd, past the Hollywood Bowl, through the Barham pass to the studio. Her feet were swollen and blistered, but she still managed to put on her high heels and a smile to give the *Wheel* audience a good show. It was around this time I heard Susan got into a bad car accident, when she swerved and crashed hard into gossip queen Rona Barrett's mailbox.

She limped home with broken ribs and severe bruises. I asked her why she didn't wait for an ambulance. It was then she told me she had been going through a wild phase, well-documented in her autobiography, *Stop the Wheel, I Want to Get Off!* I had no idea she was having such struggles.

Susan was the first woman to be nominated for an Emmy as a co-host on a game show, but she knew, in her heart, it was time to make a change. So, much to the surprise of just about everyone, she quit her job in television and moved to Texas to work with a leading cancer researcher. Susan then worked alongside President Carter's sister Ruth Carter Stapleton helping cancer patients. From there, she went to India to work with Mother Teresa's nuns. Susan was good friends with the actor Rock Hudson and was with him at his bedside during his final hours, offering him spiritual guidance. Susan returned to school to earn multiple degrees in nutrition, an M.A. in clinical psychology, and a Ph.D. in clinical psychology-all while working in television again as an executive alongside her new sweetheart, Dan Enright.

Susan has done it all. She knows just about everyone in town and can get anyone on the phone at any time. She's the female version of the "Six Degrees of Kevin Bacon" game. Susan and I have remained friends for decades and have worked on a few projects together. She has this uncanny way of calling me out of the blue when I've been grappling with a crisis. It is little wonder that she continues her good deeds as Chaplain, and through her Wheel of Grace Unlimited foundation, Susan can often be seen on the front lines, comforting the families and survivors of tragic events.

You never know where your talents will take you. Susan's often been asked if she has any regrets about her decision to leave *Wheel*. Her standard answer is, "No, except for the paycheck."

Chapter Eight

YOU HAVE TO ASK

I was assigned to work on a new sitcom. The star of the show, let's call him Jake, was blindingly handsome with the brightest, whitest smile I had ever seen. Jake was manly, despite the fact he was wearing loads of makeup and had a ton of product in his shoulder-length hair. Jake was also thoughtful, making a point of opening the door for me as we headed into the studio. It would be the first, but not the last, encounter I would have with Jake.

The production company held a little party after the taping, on the Friday before the Christmas break. Sometimes these parties were held in the ballrooms of fancy hotels (thank you, Mark Goodson). In this case, it was held in a rehearsal hall, resplendent with crepe paper Christmas and Hanukkah decorations, twelve-foot-long sandwiches, salads, desserts, and lots of adult beverages. The Pages were rarely invited to events held by the production companies, although we did sometimes forage for food once the parties were over. But this time was different. As I was leaving for the night, Jake said, "You're going to be at the Christmas party, aren't you?"

Me? I thought. "Of course," I said, never one to miss a party. So, I went back to the Page lounge, freshened up, and held my head high as I was welcomed into the next level of the show biz hierarchy.

When I arrived, most of the folks were already a few drinks ahead of me. I wanted to network with the writers and their assistants, but they were too far gone by the time I got there (and so was most of the food). I stayed for what I considered a polite amount of time, then headed back to my car for my late-night drive home. I heard the distinct sound of footsteps running up from behind me. It was Jake, wondering why I had left so early. I was afraid I had offended him and explained I had a long commute and needed to get home. We chatted a bit. He asked how I liked being a Page, and said he admired how I balanced my work and college, and soon we were making out in the back seat of my little four-door Toyota Corona. The smell of his greasepaint and the roar of our breathing made for a most unexpected end to the workday. Unexpected for me, but probably not for Jake.

I imagine he had his fair share of fair ladies with the same scenario over the years. But this was something new for me. I was brought up in the post-Doris Day, mid-Marlo Thomas, current-Gloria Steinem era of womanhood. Sure, I had taken my share of Feminist Studies classes at Cal State Northridge and subscribed to Ms. Magazine, but damn, Jake stuck his tongue down my throat, and it was good! How was I going to handle the sexual tension in the workplace? Was I going to be cool, act like it was no big deal, or start driving by his house to see if he was dating anyone else? Dating? No, we just made out, so cool is how I behaved.

The next time I saw Jake, he picked me up, swung me around, and asked me to accompany him to another holiday party. It was in Westlake Village, a relatively new upper-middle-class planned community with a man-made lake on the Los Angeles/Ventura County border. I had to work that day and needed time to change into evening clothes, so I met Jake at the party, which took place in a magnificent home. Jake, even without makeup, was still breathtakingly charismatic. He did all the right things, pulling my chair out, offering to get me a drink, and telling those gathered how smart and funny I was. Could my fling really become a thing?

We snuck away from the others and walked along the wharf where the residents had their small sailboats docked. It was a clear night, a little chilly, but Jake had taken his coat off and put it around my shoulders as we snuggled against each other, laughing and telling each other our life stories.

Jake got the naughty idea that we should sneak onto one of the boats and get to know each other a little better. He didn't have to ask me twice as I helped him untie the knots holding the canvas tarp down. Score! I was so glad I had invested in the shimmering nude pair of matching bra and panties from Lily of France. There is nothing better than sneaky sex outdoors with a guy your parents would never approve of! We tore each other's clothes off, my lips pressing against some part of his body, my fingers laced in the perfect amount of chest hair on his chiseled torso.

I wanted him more than anyone I had ever been with. He wasn't a boy. He was a man. He pressed me against the white padded seats, exploring my body, making quick haste of my pretty undergarments. Did he even notice they matched? Just before we did the deed, I looked down to admire his manhood, the most magnificent I had ever seen.

I was so ready. He was so ready! Our banging action made waves, literally. I lay splayed across the boat, water splashing into my face and onto my body as though it was an accelerant to what was already a passionate fuckfest. What was this? I think I spent too much time thinking about it, but I think it was good. We finished in a pile of sweat and wet clothes strewn all over the bottom of the boat. We laughed as we put our cold, damp clothes back on and secured the tarp to the boat. It's the only time I didn't get seasick on a boat.

I departed feeling as though I had arrived. Great sex with a hunky guy! That's what we called them back then, hunky. I drove home that night with the heater blasting in my car, feeling a bit sore and a bit like a guy who got made by the Mafia. I was in the club now. I was officially a liberated woman!

A few days later, Jake was honored for his philanthropic work, having raised a good deal of money for a children's charity. The event took place at The Beverly Wilshire Hotel, the site made famous many years later in the movie Pretty Woman. I had never been to such an upscale venue, but had always heard about it and was excited when he asked me to be his date. I said yes before my brain could stop me. What was I getting into? This night sounded above my pay grade. I was making $1.90 an hour and I didn't have the right clothes. So, I shopped the thrift stores and found the perfect LBD – Little Black Dress. Then I spent money I didn't have on a pair of shoes with a matching purse. What is it about me and matching? They were made from eel skin, a dark magenta color that could be worn with any outfit.

Jake was running late and asked me to meet him at the venue. I parked down the street because I couldn't afford the valet parking fee. I walked into the ballroom, and it was filled with grown-ups, real live adults who dressed in nice suits, the women in diamonds. Tablecloths covered beautifully decorated tables with our names written in calligraphy at the place settings. Seated to my left was an older, retired Marine who wore his uniform, covered in medals. We made small talk until Jake arrived.

Then, Jake entered the ballroom to a round of thunderous applause. He was the Man of the Hour. The Marine and I stood up, clapping as he approached the table. Jake pulled the chair out for the woman seated next to him to his right. He then sat next to me and said, "Shelley, I'd like you to meet my wife, Tammy."

In what seemed like an eternity, I extended my hand to Tammy and somehow managed to eke out the phrase, "You must be so proud of Jake tonight." She smiled the smile of a wife completely clueless that her husband, in addition to being a philanthropist, was a philanderer.

I couldn't eat, but I could gush all over the Marine. I danced with him, threw my head back and laughed, sat in a corner, and talked to him, knowing full well that Jake was watching my every move. Friends got up to speak, dignitaries presented him with plaques, and the whole time I knew Jake had some sick fantasy as to how I would congratulate him that evening.

After a round of glad-handing, beaming with pride, plaques in hand, Jake finally came over to me. I put my cheek next to his and said, "You never told me you were married." He pulled away, putting his free hand on my face, and said, "You have to ask." I turned on my new, expensive eel-skin heels and walked out of the room, never to see Jake again.

Sure, I have regrets. The thought that lingers is knowing I could have parked with the valet because, as I learned, the event would have covered the cost of the parking.

Chapter Nine

BREAK A LEG

When I signed on the dotted line to become a Page, I had no idea how fast that time would fly. We were all given eighteen months to figure out how to get off Page staff and on with our lives. My friend Lesa Lindsay, an aspiring actress from Kentucky, talked me into going with her to the World Famous Comedy Store to audition for a new improvisational theater troupe. So we headed to the Sunset Strip.

The Mother of the Comedy Store, Mitzi Shore, was fully aware of the success of *Saturday Night Live* and performing groups like Second City and The Groundlings. So she assembled a group of some of her funniest performers for auditions in the Main Room of The Store. Luckily, we saw Robin Williams there. Lesa and I had become friends with him when he worked on the ill-fated 1976 reboot of *Laugh-In* at NBC. Good, at least I knew someone other than Lesa. The only other person who stood out was Toad, The Mime, whose real name is Toni Attell. She'd worked with everyone from Marcel Marceau, who didn't speak, to Harvey Lembeck, who never stopped talking. Toad conducted the audition as other comics sat with their arms folded, waiting for the funny to happen.

Lesa signed in on the audition sheet and asked me to do the same. I didn't have a headshot or résumé, as I had no desire to be an actress, let alone a comic. I intended to be a career woman, with my eye on running NBC sometime in the not-too-distant future. At the time, realistically, for every Elayne Boosler at The Comedy Store, dozens of male comics competed for time to perform in the Main Room. It was a bastion of testosterone with comedians like David Letterman, Jay Leno, Andy Kaufman, Larry Miller, Jimmie "J J" Walker, and just about every comic you'd see on *The Tonight Show*.

I can't remember what Lesa did for her audition, but I do remember how well I did and what I did. That's because I was able to work with

Robin. He smiled and welcomed me to the stage, wearing his rainbow-colored suspenders, his hands folded in front of him. We were asked to improvise, to come up with dialogue right off the top of our heads, no script. Toni asked us to do a scene about things that annoy us. Robin started the scene. At first, I just watched him flailing his arms wildly and transforming from character to character. It didn't take long before he was sweating heavily through his t-shirt. I sensed it was my turn to jump in and do something. What could I possibly do? With a twinkle in his eye, Robin gave me a look like, "Come on. Let's play." It was as though I got hit with an electric shock to my brain. Suddenly, I had no fear, and matched Robin's frantic energy as though we were in a fencing duel. At a certain point, I remember quoting a line Richard Dreyfus said in the 1977 film *The Goodbye Girl.* It was something like, "I don't like the panties drying on the rod." It cracked Robin up, and I had fun. When we were done, he gave me a hairy, sweaty hug.

The next day, I got the call, but Lesa didn't. I had been asked to join "The Comedy Store Players." This was huge! First, because my dear friend, Lesa, didn't make the cut. I was disappointed and felt awful for her. Secondly, this was now a significant detour in my career path. I would have to quit being a Page to rehearse and perform with this elite group of comics. I told Toni I would think about it and get back to her the next day. The next day proved fateful.

Sure, it was a chance of a lifetime, but also, it involved a lot of risks and no cash. Dorothy, a former Air Force nurse with a brown cigarette always firmly wedged between her fingers, prepared the weekly schedule for the 100ish Pages. I asked her if she would be able to weasel-waggle my Page schedule to work only days, so I wouldn't have to quit my dream job to support my evening folly. As you can imagine, that didn't go over well. I left work that evening more confused than ever. I joined some friends to hear their opinions on what I should do. To get my mind off my dilemma, we played a little ping-pong, and about a half-hour into the game, I tripped on a loose tile and crashed on to the hard floor, breaking my leg. Hello, Universe? Did I need a bigger sign? I thought the old show biz adage "Break a Leg" was supposed to mean good luck?

It was now utterly impractical, if not impossible, to quit my job. I would need to keep my medical insurance until I completed physical therapy so I could resume my Page duties. There was no way I could join an insanely wacky troupe of zany, brilliant, hysterical...oh, why do I continue to torture myself with what might have been? I told Toni what happened and wasn't offered the opportunity to come back when I had healed.

Instead, my break gave me a break from giving tours and ushering for the shows at NBC. I was given a desk job, and a brief internship in the Story Department. I read scripts, novels, magazines, anything that NBC might be able to option and develop into a two-hour movie or miniseries. I was glad to be employed, but I was also feeling pretty sorry for myself. I was such a company gal that to pass the time, I sent off for a do-it-yourself hook rug kit. It featured the old RCA logo of Nipper, The Dog listening to a Victrola, hearing "His Master's Voice." There is nothing like wearing a big plaster cast in the middle of a hot summer in beautiful downtown Burbank with a wool hook rug on your lap to crush one's spirits.

A woman working full-time as one of the readers, Janet Greek, became my unwitting mentor shortly after I began the internship. To improve my office skills, I decided to take a shorthand class at Cal State Northridge. Two days into the course, I realized I had made a colossal mistake. I was so demoralized. I couldn't understand all those squiggles and accent marks. Why didn't people make an audio recording of what they needed and transcribe it later? It was such an obvious way to do business. How would I be able to progress up the corporate ladder without learning shorthand? Janet saw me sobbing at my desk and asked me why I was so upset. Her words of comfort have guided me all these decades later, "If you don't want to do something for a living, never learn how to do it." Mind blown! Did I want to be an assistant? No! Did Dick Ebersol know shorthand? No! A few months later, Janet would be instrumental in me getting my first job off the Page staff and into the NBC corporate world. It wasn't because I was the best candidate for the job. It was because she was dating the Vice President I went to work with, and she knew I wouldn't fool around with him and could keep an eye on any other females who might be lurking.

A broken leg also meant I'd have to give up my favorite Sunday summertime activity of playing on the NBC co-ed softball team, which I named "The Not Ready for Prime Time Players," as an homage to the original SNL cast members. Truth be told, I was a bit of a ringer. I was good at playing second base because I could accurately throw to home plate. It was fun watching the opposing team move closer to the infield when I was at bat. Not only was I a short female, but I also batted right-handed, so they all anticipated an easy out. The joke was on them as I could pull the ball into left field, assuring myself at least a base hit. Now, I'd be relegated to being the team's scorekeeper.

My broken leg also made me think I'd have to give up the highlight of my summer, but my Page Pal George Glovna came through like a champ. Every summer, I'd go to The Greek Theater, a 6,000-seat amphitheater on the grounds of Griffith Park, to enjoy the work of musician, storyteller, balladeer, and humanitarian Harry Chapin. And every year, I'd wear the same bright orange t-shirt I purchased at my first Chapin concert. It reads, "You Can Always Count on The Cheap Seats," a nod to Harry's loyal and devoted fans who couldn't afford the pricier tickets. But, George, like the outstanding softball player he was, came through in a clutch and somehow managed to score two tickets, front row center, for a Sunday night under the stars to see Harry perform.

I hobbled my way to our seats and promptly propped my leg up on a brass guardrail to settle in for a hot July night. We smiled and sang along to Harry's most enduring songs, *"The Cat's in the Cradle," "Taxi," and "WOLD."* As he always did, Harry finished the concert with a group sing-along of *"Circle."* Harry reached down and handed the microphone to George, who rose to the challenge and sang a few lyrics. Who said good things don't happen to good people? I was thrilled for George! It meant more to me emotionally than I knew I needed.

The next night, July 30, 1978, I was thrilled to see Harry was the musical guest on *The Tonight Show.* I alerted George, and when the taping ended, we made a mad dash backstage. We had to tell Harry how much we enjoyed his performance that evening of *"Poor Damn Fool"* as much as we did at his concert the night before. But before we could say anything, Harry took one look at the cast on my leg, pointed to it, stared me in the eyes, and laughed, exclaiming, "You were at my show last night!" And like a superhero, I proudly ripped open my white Page blouse to reveal my bright orange t-shirt with Harry's slogan. We laughed together, and I was able to thank him for the many years of inspiration and entertainment he'd given me.

Harry was right. All my life was a circle. I was right back in the Page ranks, hoping to find a job within the next few months that would allow me to learn more, meet more people, and take that next step up the corporate ladder. The Comedy Store gig was my chance to grab the brass ring, and I missed it. It could have been that job outside of NBC that Dick Ebersol advised me to take. Leave and come back later for big bucks. I've played the woulda, shoulda, coulda game a million times in my head. Well, onward and sideways!

The gift I did receive from my "Break A Leg" phase was to have spoken to Harry. And no one can take that away from me. He was gone three years later, killed on the Long Island Expressway. The epitaph on his marker reads, *"Oh if a man tried, To take his time on Earth, And prove before he died, What one man's life could be worth, I wonder what would happen, to this world."* I guess I was lucky, after all.

NBC Burbank Page Staff, September 1976. I'm the shortest one, second row, 4th from the right, with the sunglasses on the top of my head that look like Mickey Mouse ears.

The Famous Floyd Photo Front Row: Charlie Coon, Middle Row Left to Right: Cindy Tanaka, Me (next to Floyd Jackson) Tim Jones, Dinah Brein, Risé Irushalmi. Back Row Left to Right: Pete Hammond, Jim McDonald, Tom Hansen.

December 1976. I almost killed James Stewart! This photo was taken in the NBC Midway. Hours later, I was rushed to the hospital with mononucleosis and Hepatitis A.

Circle gets the square! The original host of *The Hollywood Squares*, Peter Marshall, and Me at the premiere of the 2017 Rose Marie documentary, *Wait for Your Laugh.*

Pages on a Press Junket, 1976. From Left to Right: Melissa Hunt, Actor Ben Murphy, Carrie Estrada, Wendi Larson, and Beth Rees.

I accompanied *CHiPs* star Erik Estrada on his press tour. We got off to a bit of a rough start. Months later, this photo turned up in a magazine.

Gilda Radner seated with Page Linda Levinson. Gilda asked Pete Hammond, Melissa Hunt, and Linda to take her on a quickie tour of Hollywood that became a legendary Page story.

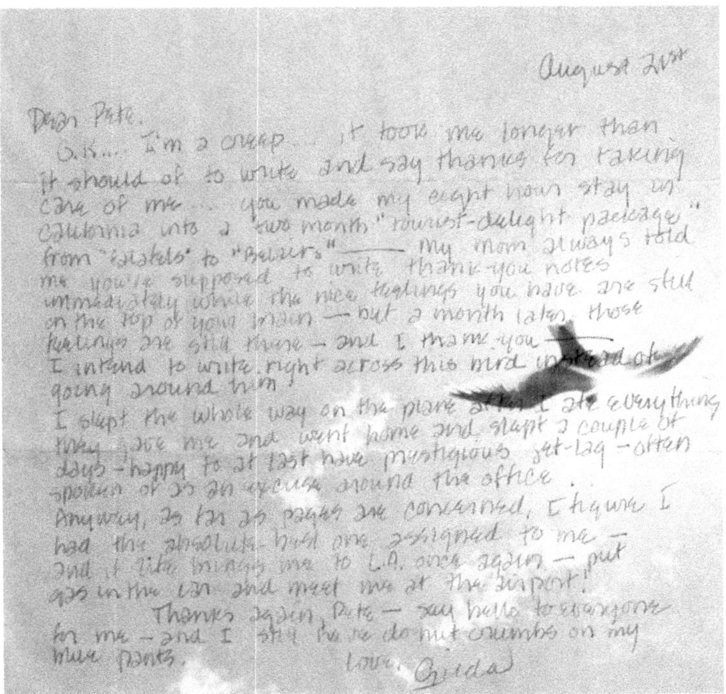

Gilda Radner's Funny Thank You Note

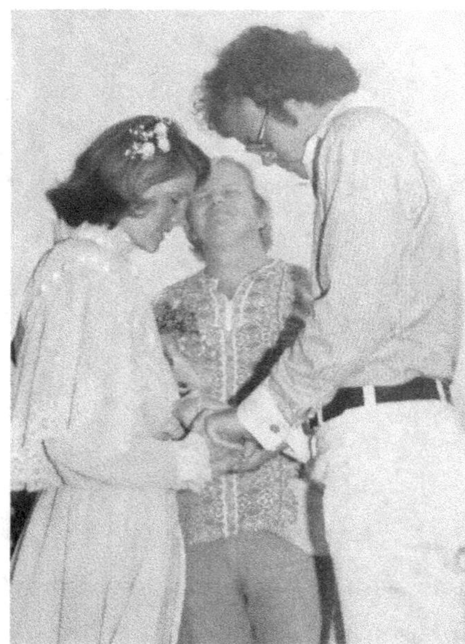

Following a whirlwind romance, Original *Wheel of Fortune* hostess Susan Stafford wed NBC Executive Dick Ebersol on the beach in Malibu on July 4, 1976. The marriage was later annulled.

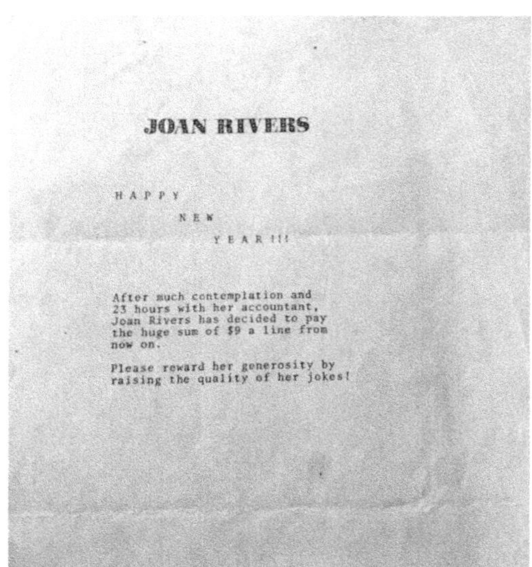

Can we joke? A few Pages tried to earn a little money by submitting jokes to Joan Rivers. Eventually, Linda Levinson got a raise and a personalized letter from Joan.

Mr. Jim McDonald

January 5, 1978

Dear Jim:

Thanks for sending along the photographs of
Art Fern and Father Time to me. I enjoyed
seeing them and will be framing them for the
office.

Best wishes,

Johnny Carson

Here's...a Johnny Carson thank you note to Jim McDonald for going beyond the call of duty.

Actor McLean Stevenson could often be seen roaming the hallways. Here he is posing Linda Levinson and a few Pages in their civilian clothes for a promotional photo against the elephant doors of Studio 4, home of *Chico and the Man.*

To plan each episode of *Liar's Club*, Larry Hovis put a description of each item under consideration on an index card and affixed them to a bulletin board.

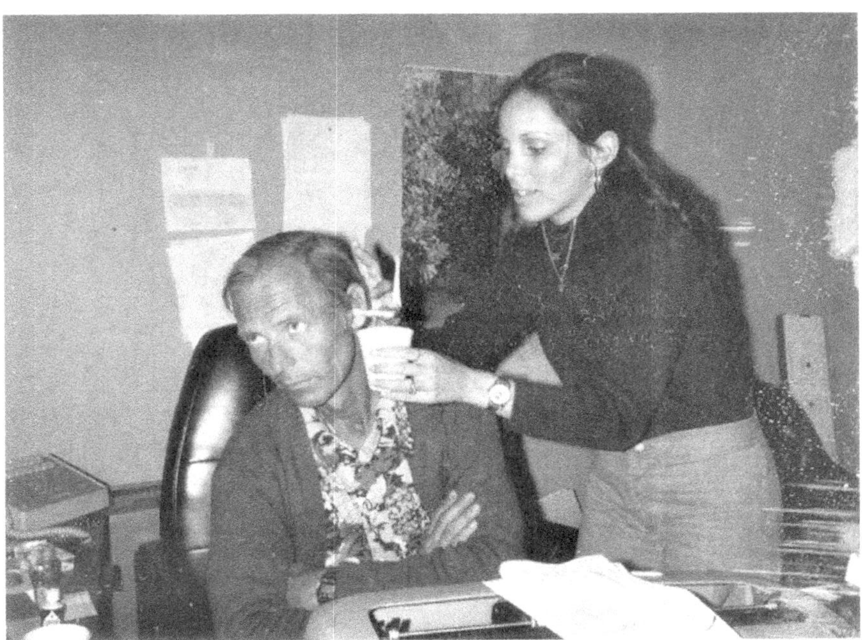

From *Liar's Club* testing lab, Larry was the guinea pig when I lit one end of an item sent in by a home viewer, an ear wax wicker.

Betty White would often bring her mother, Tess White, to the tapings of *Liar's Club*, hosted by her son-in-law, Allen Ludden.

I'm standing next to Redd Foxx's lucky charm, Sadie O'Sullivan, along with my Page pal, Cindy Hain. Sadie told me she was Jewish and was only married to O'Sullivan long enough to have a baby, then divorced him.

The 1977 Primetime Emmy Awards was a night to remember and one of the best nights of my life.

Chuck Barris sent someone who plucked me off a tour and onto *The Gong Show*.

I'm seated with Chuck's daughter, Della, who reminded me of me when I was a teenager.

Chuck Barris

Hanging out at the Chuck Barris Production offices doing game show run-thrus was always a treat and a lot of fun. I adored Chuck.

I met Chuck in 1972 when I was still a student at Agoura High School. I did two episodes of *The Dating Game*.

A man loved and loathed, but mostly loved, Jay Michelis. His unconventional managerial style would not be welcome today.

A ticket, preserved in Lucite, from the final taping of *The Tonight Show Starring Johnny Carson* courtesy of the Bruce Rubinstein Collection.

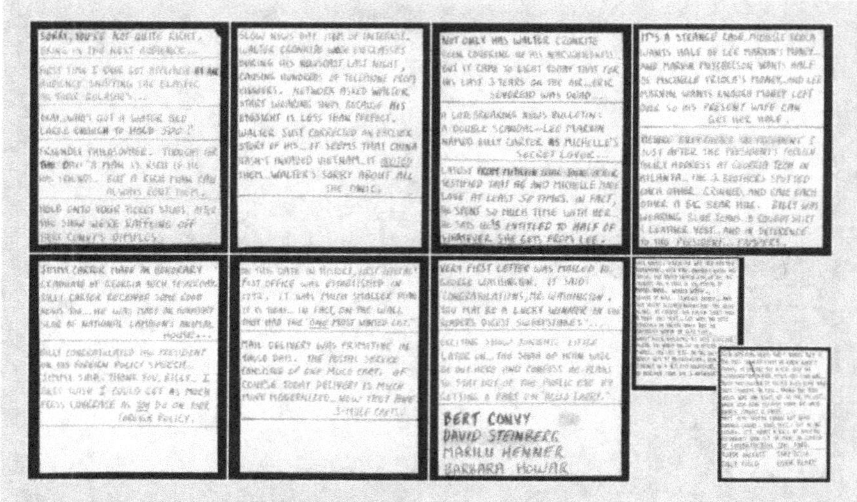

From February 21, 1979: Johnny's monologue cue cards. As you can see, the jokes were not written out in full sentences.

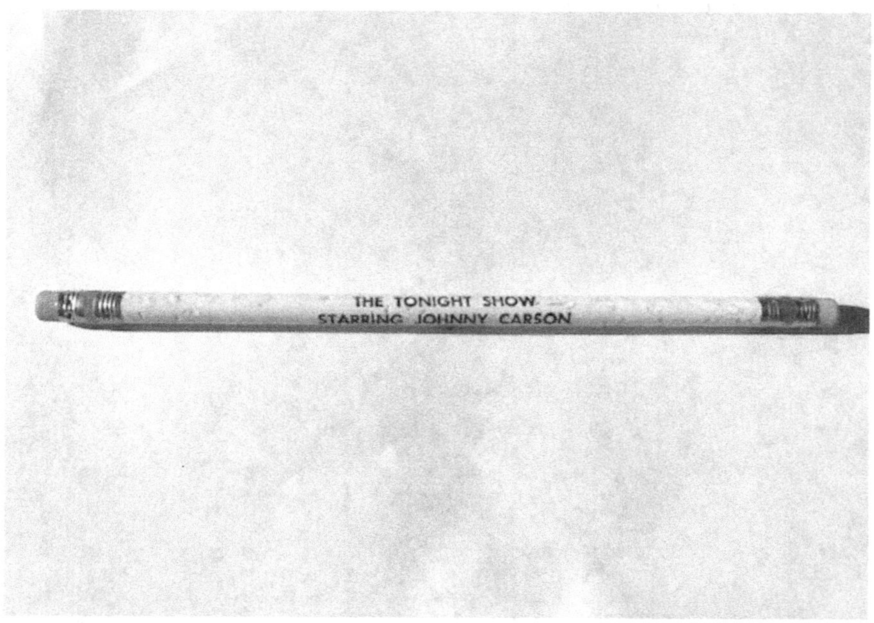

A slightly dented double-headed pencil from the desk of Johnny Carson. Johnny would drum along to the performance of the musical guests and the NBC Orchestra fronted by Doc Severinsen.

The former Page Subterranean Lounge was turned into an office/dressing room and escape room for Johnny Carson. He made his final exit from the building from the door on the left.

Johnny walked through this tunnel, under the midway, into the administration building, then out to a waiting helicopter that took his wife Alexis Maas and him to their home in Malibu for a cast and crew wrap party.

Halloween 1978 when the always sartorial splendid Courtney Conte dressed as NBC's new President, Fred Silverman.

Being the true-blue employee when I dressed as The NBC Peacock.

When in Rome: Trying to pay it forward, I treated a guy I thought was a starving assistant to a visit to The Vatican. I later learned he was an actor, Grant Show.

Page Adjacent friend Steve Goldstein was able to chat a bit with Paul McCartney and get his autograph backstage at *The Tonight Show*. Photo courtesy of Steve Goldstein.

Decades after leaving California, Linda (Levinson) Taylor came to town for a visit, and we all picked up right where we left off. Left to right: Linda, Pete Hammond, Me, Al Ovadia at Art's Deli in Studio City, CA

Another Page gathering that included (left to right) Gregg Moscoe, Me, Courtney Conte, Linda (Levinson) Taylor, Melissa (Hunt) Trikilis, and Pete Hammond

A snapshot on the stairs at the annual Madelyn and Pete Hammond Christmas Party. From the left going, up the stairs: Sandy (Crompton) Selma, Roxanne (Yamaguchi) Moster, Dinah Brein, Renee Palyo, Brian Robinette, Debbi Pettit, Tim Danker. Right Side: Me, Jim McDonald, and Pete Hammond.

Former Page Tom Chasuk and I co-hosted shows in Los Angeles on TalkRadio 790KABC-AM. Our good friend, Richard Hack (Center,) was one of our best guests.

My friend, agent, and game show historian, Fred Wostbrock, on the set of *Supermarket Sweep* taped at NBC Burbank. It took 24 years, but I finally got my own office on the lot!

Marc Summers worked at NBC on the game show *Celebrity Sweepstakes* when I was a Page, but we didn't meet until decades later when, while I was interviewing for a writing job with him, I told Marc a trivia question he was given to read while hosting a show wrong. I got the job and a wonderful lifelong friend.

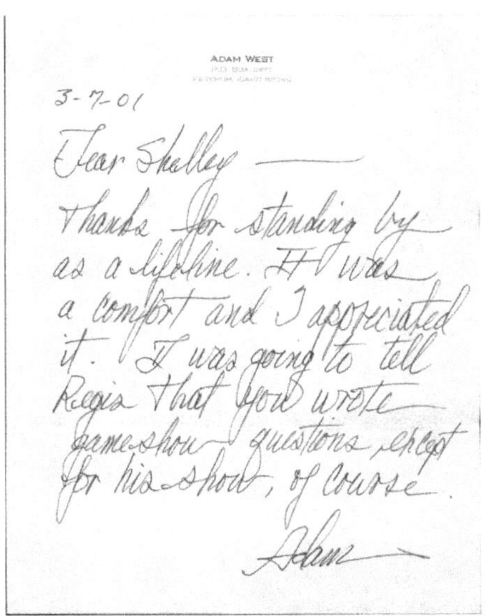

I came to the rescue of Batman! Adam West asked me to be one of his lifelines when he played *Who Wants To Be A Millionaire.*

Time it was and what a time it was. An unofficial Page Reunion in the Fall of 2019 at the home of Renee Palyo.

Chapter Ten

SIDE HUSTLES & TALKING TRASH

The more industrious Pages found ways to get a few perks out of possessing tickets to NBC's most popular TV show tapings. Some told me they made arrangements with the hotels in the area to swap TV show tickets for free hotel rooms. That worked out nicely when a group of us spent a free weekend at a new resort in Palm Springs that a grateful businessman had comped. Much to my shock and surprise, a Page told me he had worked a deal where he waited for a designated limo to pull up. The driver would hand him a wad of cash in exchange for tickets to that evening's taping of *The Tonight Show.*

For a brief time, NBC set up a satellite ticket office at The World Famous Chinese Theatre in Hollywood. A popular tourist destination, its courtyard is covered in cement and features the hand and footprints of current and iconic movie stars. Only male Pages were assigned to this gig, working 6:00 – 10:00 p.m. Some saw this as being assigned to Page purgatory, stuck hawking free tickets to tourists to some of our less popular shows. And you would have to repeatedly explain to tourists how to get tickets to *The Tonight Show* because they weren't available at that booth.

Sometimes, having a long-time NBC employee as your father can backfire on you. Courtney Conte's dad, Gino was the Director of Production Services and an all-around great guy. He never interfered with his son's career trajectory. "My dad said, I'm not going to help you," Courtney told me.

At this time, Tom Gough was in charge of the Page staff, and he treated Courtney differently than the other staff members. "Tom Gough wanted to be a unit manager so badly. My dad thought he was an idiot and never made him a Unit Manager, so he punished me for seven months by sending me to the Chinese Theatre. Every day! I was twenty, and he said I couldn't work on shows until I was twenty-one. He said it was a new rule. I said I was about to graduate and I can learn fast. He punished me. Guest Relations Vice President Jay Michalis knew about it. He said, 'Just be patient.'"

Courtney soon realized that having a satellite office away from the NBC mothership had its advantages: "That was a fun assignment. I would sneak Pages in all the time through the back door right up to the private balcony. I'd get manicures, and I'd go to the Cowboy Shoeshine Stand. One day, I saw this amazon walking around, and it was (actress and supermodel) Margot Hemingway. I dated her a few times."

Tom Hansen loved the opportunity to work off-site because that meant no tours! And, as Tom went on to say, he shared his good fortune with his friends. "It would come up in the rotation for me about once a month. *Star Wars* was playing at the theatre. The back door of the ticket booth made it easy to walk through a small hallway to the theatre's lobby. I remember calling my fraternity brothers when I was going to be assigned to the booth, and there would always be a group of about six of them who would show up at the back door, and I would get them in the theatre to enjoy *Star Wars* for free."

Another advantage of working on a television pilot or series was the wrap party. It was the time when the cast and crew patted each other on the back and promised to be friends forever. At the time, people really meant it. But unfortunately, unless a concerted effort was made, the people you spent twelve to fourteen hours a day with for weeks or months, people who became family, soon scattered to the wind. I knew early on the Pages I met on the job had to stay in my life. Thankfully a core group of us have remained friends.

Wrap parties could be anything from a few deli platters to a full-on catered feast. It was customary to have a DJ blasting the latest dance music, and mirrored disco balls reflecting colorful party lights while cast and crew gathered to get down and get funky. The vibe of the parties could vary. If the cast and crew knew the show has been picked up for another season, great! Everyone was happy. The booze was flowing, and the conversation lively. If there were an uncertain future, people would still show up, hoping to be included if another batch of shows was ordered, but then leave before the party started winding down. Those who purposely stayed late weren't usually looking for a date. Their gaze was fixed on the unused items from the snack table, known as craft services. I've seen executives fill the trunks of their cars with cases of water, soft drinks, and snacks before leaving the lot for what might be the last time.

Another tradition to the end of the season was the SWAG, short for "Stuff We All Get." Long before you could order everything on eBay or Amazon, only cast and crew members could wear satin jackets with a show's logo or sip endless cups of coffee from a mug bearing the show's name (and often personalized with the employee's name). If a Page were fortunate to be assigned to a show for the entire season, they would get the goodies, too.

Tom Hansen was invited to an exclusive wrap party by John Belushi. It was to be held at the Universal City Studios amphitheater, where he would perform with Dan Ackyrod as The Blues Brothers. It turned out to be a huge disappointment when Belushi, stiff as a board and stoned out of his mind, had to be carried off the stage in a cart.

Somehow, I managed to score an invitation to a wrap party at a private home in Coldwater Canyon. My friend Julian drove, and we were excited because rumor had it all the *Saturday Night Live* people would be there. At last! My chance to rub my polyester-covered elbows with the hottest stars on TV. There was also the promise of a mountain of cocaine. We hung around for about two hours, not knowing a soul. I tried to hobnob with the NBC New York contingent, but all eyes were focused on who was coming through the front door, not who was actually in the house. Just as I was getting bored and wanted to leave, the guest of honor arrived: the mountain of cocaine. The coke, tightly wrapped in what looked like a five-pound bag of sugar, was poured onto a glass-top coffee table. There was a feeding frenzy as people dove onto the table, pushing, shoving and snorting. I turned to Julian and said, "We have to get the hell out of here!" He completely disagreed, wanting to party. All I could think of was the cops breaking down the door and busting everyone, and I'd be back to working for Sears if they would even have me. Julian was snow-blind, so I left. It was well past midnight, and there I was, walking two and a half miles down the dark and winding Coldwater Canyon Drive to the Beverly Hills Hotel. I took my high heels off at about mile one. So by the time I reached the hotel, my stockings were torn, and my feet were filthy, covered with sticky pine needles, making me look like a Yeti in a blue blazer. Thankfully, I found a payphone (cell phones weren't a thing yet, called a cab, and beat myself up all the way home, knowing I had just missed my chance to be best friends with all the *Saturday Night Live* people. When Julian and I were speaking again, he told me the *Saturday Night Live* people never showed up, and the party broke up shortly, or should I say snortly, after I left.

One of the sweetest Pages I worked with, was originally from a small town in Texas, and had a unique way of earning some extra cash. For several days and nights, she listened nonstop to a country music station from Los Angeles. They had a contest where they played music for several days with no commercials. When they finally ran a commercial, the first listener to call would win cash. I can't remember the exact amount, but it was thousands, perhaps as much as $10,000. She stayed awake for days, and, sure enough, around 4:00 a.m., she was the first caller and won the cash! I remember she was a bit embarrassed when she told me about her winnings because it somehow went against her work ethic. I thought it was a great idea. Years later, during a Writers Guild strike, when I was broke, I copied her strategy to win cash and gift certificates from radio stations and TV shows.

Crazy Jay, a good-looking surfer-type guy with a constant smile, was able to make a few connections with the casting people at *Days of Our Lives* and picked up some acting work between Page assignments. He also worked as a flight attendant for the now-defunct Western Airlines, where he is best remembered for jumping out of a jet just as it was pulling away from the terminal because he realized he was on the wrong flight.

Then there was Leisure Lenny, who one day pulled up to the Guest Relations office in a luxury convertible shortly after he was hired onto the

Page staff. That could only have meant one of two things: Either his parents gave him cash to survive; or, as in this case, he became the resident Dr. Feelgood. He scored bags of Quaaludes, cocaine, and marijuana for the executives and talent. Keep in mind; this was the mid-1970s when no one thought these drugs were addictive, just a lot of fun and highly illegal.

Linda Levinson, a Page who started a few months before me, was an aspiring comedy writer, and she even tried her hand a few times at stand-up, performing on open mic night at The Comedy Store in Westwood Village. Linda was able to meet Joan Rivers and began submitting jokes to her. "Joan would be on the three-for-one plan. She would buy three, then stole the fourth." Joan was always up for new material. Alan Burnett wrote jokes for her, too. I even sold a few jokes to Joan. Joan reminded me of a hummingbird, always in motion, going from one person to the next. When I finally got the nerve to ask her if I could submit jokes to her, she stopped, pointed her finger at me, and said, "Have them ready the next time I'm here. If they're good, I'll buy them." And what was Joan's going rate for selling her a joke, a joke you couldn't turn around and sell to anyone else or use yourself? Linda and I were paid $7 per joke. Linda got a raise and showed me the letter she'd kept all these years, written on Joan Rivers' personal stationery, increasing Linda's rate to $9 a joke as long as she could increase the "quality" of her material.

I took on a little writing task, too. The tour itself was lacking something for the school children. They were too young to attend the show's taping, so I approached Eba with the idea of a special tour written for elementary school-aged kids to get a taste of a TV experience while on tour. No one in Guest Relations saw it as a problem, but I saw it as an opportunity to make my bones on the staff and get a little something extra on my woefully lacking résumé. And, to sweeten the pot, I said I would do it for free on my own time, so what did they have to lose? Keep in mind, this was years before people owned home video cameras and cassette players. So, the mystery and magic of television were still a big lure to parents and children.

To my utter delight, my script was accepted and incorporated into the tour when school groups were there. It was rudimentary, at best. The storyline was simple and involved a showdown at a cowboy saloon. The kids were given cardboard boxes that looked like cameras featuring the NBC logo, as well as a few wardrobe pieces, props, fake food, and a working applause sign. It was the best I could do...or the most the management would do. The pièce de résistance was when we brought out the breakaway bottles made of lightweight sugar glass. Frankly, it was all the kids really wanted to see, but they had to endure my little play before the bad guy got clobbered. For insurance purposes, we had the kids vote on which Page would hit him or herself over the head with the breakaway bottle. It was the first show I'd written and produced for NBC, and I had a blast doing it for the kids. The kid's show was added to the NBC company brochure as one of the fun things to do while touring the facility. I was proud as a peacock and viewed it as my first professional writing gig...for NBC, no less! And, I learned a valuable lesson: In show biz, if you work for free, you can work all the time.

A few times a year, I would volunteer to help at a celebrity charity fundraiser at a private country club in Tarzana. It was fun, and it gave me a chance to hang with some of the NBC big shots. I drove a hospitality golf cart filled with water, soft drinks, and beer, always careful not to drive off the hilly, winding paths throughout the course. Fred de Cordova and *The Tonight Show* director Bobby Quinn were both golfers, and they remembered my name once we were back in Burbank. I let the men know there was more to me than just ushering and being a tour guide. I was philanthropic!

Perhaps the most infamous story that still circulates among the Pages was when a woman was waiting in line to see *The Tonight Show*. She approached two male Pages, wanting to meet the show's executive producer, Fred de Cordova. In reality, we had little to no access to Fred except for the occasional polite nod or wave in the hallway. After the taping, the male Pages brought her backstage to an empty dressing room, and, as the story goes, she allegedly performed oral sex on both Pages to get some face time with Fred. I know the two Pages who are rumored to have done this. I believe, one did not do it, and the other probably did it all the time!

Michael D. had a side hustle giving haircuts to the Pages, and damn, he did have a great head of hair! In what became one of the most *Twilight Zone* moments in our Page circle, Roxanne and Tim turned one of their regular dinners into a life altering experience for Michael D. They were at the small bistro Yellowfingers in Sherman Oaks, CA and commented on how much their server looked like Michael D.: he was tall, lean, dark-haired, and shared the same crooked smile. As they were paying the check, Roxanne Yamaguchi and Tim Danker approached the young man and told him that he must have a twin because they worked with a guy who looked so much like him. "What's his last name?" the server asked. "Deats," they responded. A look came over the server's face. His mother never told him much about his birth father, but he did know his last name: Deats. It isn't a common name. So the next step was a face-to-face meeting. Michael D. was a bit reluctant, but he was finally persuaded to take a look for himself.

When the moment arrived, there was no doubt. They looked at each other and knew right away they were half-brothers. Turns out papa was a rolling stone, and while married to Michael's mother, he had an affair with the server's mother. They chatted a bit and discovered they had a lot in common, including playing the drums. They made plans to talk in a few days.

When you have 100 plus Pages working under the sizzling hot summertime conditions we experienced in Burbank, there would be conflicts, especially when several large tour groups all needed to be escorted through the building. Lunchtime was the worst time because two companies, Starline and Orange Coast Tours, dropped their wide-eyed loads off in our lobby, and we needed to show them all there was to see in one hour, so they could catch their bus to the next awe-inspiring destination. Often we'd be yelling over each other as we passed through the wardrobe and set construction areas. And, you didn't want to be the last tour group, as you'd be inundated by the stench of the oily substance that spewed from multiple demonstrations of the only special effect we had: The Fog Machine. At least these tour groups got to see something, even if they didn't see a celebrity. Since it was around lunchtime for most shows, the stages were open. We could walk in, look around, even if it was empty, and give the guests a brief history of our beloved lot. It would be fun to overhear what each Page said to their group as we passed in the halls. The midway area, where the stars parked their cars, was a good vantage point to try and spot a celebrity heading for The Hungry Peacock Commissary (often the butt of Johnny Carson's jokes.) To the south of our lot was a relatively large mountain. I'd often hear the Pages say to their tour group, "That's where the opening credits of *M*A*S*H** were filmed, or, "This is Walton's Mountain." The more creative types would tell the tourists it was the mountaintop where Julie Andrews twirled as she sang, "The hills are alive with the sound of music." All were lies, but the tourists were never the wiser and loved hearing the inside scoop.

Not long into his Pagedom, Courtney couldn't stand to look at, let alone wear, the uniforms we were all assigned. We each received two blazers, two blouses/shirts, two skirts for the women, and slacks for the men. That's right. Female Pages were not permitted to wear pants. At least it was better than the mini-skirts and white go-go boots my predecessors had to wear. Courtney, a sartorial gent to this day, went to our then Manager of the Department, Al Ovadia, with a plan. "I told Al, we're in fourth place out of three networks. We have to up our image. I called this company in Boston, Joseph Bank Clothiers, and I made a deal for about $100 a Page for two suits, something crazy like that. I negotiated the deal, and Al said that's okay. And they were all three-piece wool suits with cotton shirts. No more polyester crap, and we all looked so much better." By the time my new uniform arrived, I was long gone from the staff. Courtney was right. They looked much better. Because of his keen eye and attention to detail, Courtney caught the attention of former KNBC local news anchor Tom Snyder and the folks at *The Tomorrow Show*, the late-night talk show that followed *The Tonight Show* in most markets. Courtney's intelligence and dapper looks made him the perfect Page to work with the Snyder crew to welcome their more sophisticated guests, most of whom sat talking one-on-one with Tom in a dark, cigarette smoke-filled studio. Word soon spread that Courtney was the force behind getting better uniforms for the Pages, and Tom Snyder couldn't let that pass without a comment or two.

When Tom's guests, Helen O'Connell and Rosemary Clooney, were a last-minute cancellation because the two gals had a cold, someone on *The Tomorrow Show* staff grabbed Courtney and decided he would be the guest. "They had the first slot open," Courtney told me. "So, they all decided I was going to be the guest." Courtney, with little warning, found himself thrust in front of Snyder and started playfully making fun of the late-night host. "The first question Snyder asks me is, 'Are you a guard?' He was such a prick! I said, 'No, I'm a Page, and I actually have a college education.' The next question was, 'Explain to me what nepotism is and how you got your job?' This is live! He's going right for my throat. He asked me about why I made such a big deal about getting the Page uniforms changed, and I explained, 'I'm not into petroleum products.' It went off the rails from there:

Tom: "So tell me, you take these idiots from the Midwest on these
              stupid tours. Tell me what they do?"
Courtney: "We go by the studios where Mr. Carson..."
              Snyder volleyed back:
Tom: "Oh, you call me Tom."
Courtney: "Yeah, but he makes more money for the network than you
              do."
Tom: "So what do they ask you about on the tour?
Courtney: "Well, Tom, they mostly ask me about your hair."
              Tom was always vain about his hair, and Courtney knew
              that was the perfect zinger.
Tom (turning to the crew): "He's not a Page. He's a pusher from the
              South Bronx."
              Their bantering went on a bit longer.

Courtney went on to say, "I took his teddy bear, and we were going back and forth. I started doing (my impression of) Dan Aykroyd doing

Tom (Ha, haha, that's a fair question, sir) to him on live TV. It went on for seven minutes, and it was fucking hysterical!

"When we finished, Tom said, 'Bye Court-e, because I heard a big NBC executive calls you Court-e.' (He was referring to Dave Tebet.) If I had time to think about it, I probably would have been nervous, but they just threw me in the chair."

One of the perks of working on a Saturday was hanging around the Page Lounge to watch the East coast broadcast transmission of *Saturday Night Live* as it was being done live from New York. We could watch the show as it was happening three hours before it would air on the West coast, giving us bragging rights and the ability to watch it again later that evening. We'd watch the show most of the time and eat food from the vending machines, and occasionally, we'd have a few beers and some wine, making sure we destroyed all evidence of alcohol on the premises. After all, it was a violation of Rule #6 in the Page Manual.

Neil Weiner liked to park himself in the Page Lounge, using it as his personal office. There was only one outgoing line, and more often than not, Neil would be on it. I once overheard him tell his former USC classmate that he was "now at NBC, doing Public Relations for Rickles." He wasn't entirely telling the truth, but he wasn't lying either because when he gave his tours, he was talking up the *CPO Sharkey* series that starred Don Rickles. Neil had the gift of gab. He could charm and reason with just about anyone, including the abrasive comic Pat Cooper, who once comped a hotel room for Neil and invited him to see his show in Las Vegas.

There was one Page we all disliked. He was the Frank Burns to our *M*A*S*H** unit: a snitch, a tattletale, a total weasel, someone looking to advance his career by trying to destroy others. He was a rat, and he looked like a rat, with his scrawny little face and constant expression of disdain. His hands were even rodent-like, always bent at the wrist. The only other time I'd seen that particular posture was in the movie *Viva Las Vegas* when Ann-Margret danced with Elvis. He put his perfectly functioning fingers to use after-hours when he'd go through the trash cans in all the Guest Relations offices. That included the Page lounge, ticket department, and executive offices. He was looking for discarded memos or top-secret whatever-the-hell he thought he'd find. Soon, we began spiking the trash cans with half-eaten food and cigarette butts. Hey, if he was going to get a little dirty on us, we were going to get a little dirt on him!

Leave it to Jim McDonald to have something good come out of dumpster diving. Jim noticed the Photography Department had tossed a large stack of new pictures in a trash bin featuring Johnny Carson from various sketches he'd done on his show over the years. Jim rescued the photos and put them into an NBC interoffice envelope. Within hours, they were delivered directly to Drue Wilson, Johnny's secretary. A few days later, Jim received the call few Pages received. Mr. Carson's secretary asked if Jim could come to Johnny's office above Studio 1. Johnny wanted to thank Jim personally and followed up with a personal note:

"January 5, 1978. Dear Jim, Thank you for sending along the photographs of Art Fern and Father Time to me. I enjoyed seeing them and will be framing them for the office. Best wishes, Johnny Carson."

Chapter Eleven

QUID PRO NO & THE MASHER

Sexual harassment was alive and well (and thriving) at NBC. It wasn't just me. When talking to my Page friends, some of the men and women I worked with were also the recipients of unwanted advances from both Stars and Executives, straight and gay. Sometimes they'd follow us down to the Page lounge to make their move. Roxanne recalls the horror of introducing her parents to one of their favorite stars, Redd Foxx, only to have him "put his hands all over me. It was so embarrassing and totally inappropriate."

I lost the friendship of a Page I truly admired, Donna, because I was a fervent believer of the Girl Code: Never date another girl's boyfriend. Her then-sweetheart, Bryan, was a mid-level executive who worked in the Administration Building. A job became available in his department, an entry-level management role that I was most likely too inexperienced to get. What's the worst that could happen? I wouldn't get the job. I jumped at the chance to snag an interview. Before the appointment, I asked Donna if she planned to apply for the job, and she said no. I didn't want to get in the way of her career advancement. So with the path clear, I changed from my Page uniform to a tasteful power suit to reflect I was ready to make the leap from the Page staff to the A Building. We went into Bryan's office, where he proceeded to close the door. It was no big deal because it was a formal interview. We discussed the job's duties, how it would involve travel, and if I minded long hours. How would I handle a dispute between the network and the production company? Was I easily offended by dirty jokes? Well, a firm yes for travel. For disputes, I'd listen to both sides, then take the issue up with him. Dirty jokes? I told Bryan if I got the job, I'd make sure to tell him the jokes when I got back to his office. I was trying to be one of the boys and not let his questions throw me.

But he didn't want me to be one of the boys. Bryan wanted me to be one of his girls!

Bryan came right out and said that I would have to sleep with him if he were to recommend me for the job. Bryan was young, good-looking, and my friend's boyfriend! In a most indignant tone, I told him that I was never going to sleep with him and that I would tell his girlfriend what he had offered up to me. I was so mad at Bryan for making the job conditional and even more upset he would betray Donna.

I was sick to my stomach. What was I going to do? Go to Human Resources and say, "Bryan said I could have the job if I slept with him?" They would have fired me on the spot for causing trouble. After all, Bryan was making more money for the company than I was schlepping tourists through the building every hour.

I retreated to the Page Lounge, where I found Donna and asked if we could talk outside, away from the others. I'm guessing she expected me to fill her in on how well my interview with Bryan went. I told her the truth as to what had happened. I told her it pained me to say what happened but she should know what kind of a man she was dating. She stared at me, not saying a word, then said, "Okay," and walked away.

What did that mean? Was she marching over to his office to end it? Was she going to get his side of the story? I never found out exactly what happened, because Donna never talked to me again. I didn't know that she had moved in with Bryan two weeks earlier. And ultimately, she chose to believe him or stay with him because she loved him or whatever. So much for the Girl Code! I had upset her world, and she didn't want to be reminded of his attempted infidelity. They never married but did remain close friends. As his career declined, she worked on a top-rated NBC series, eventually rising in the ranks to become one of their executive producers. Bryan married, had a family, and passed away at a young age. To this day, I still admire Donna. I would have liked to have remained her friend. Lesson learned. Women can't always confide in each other. So, it was back to keeping quiet about the quid pro quo that eventually brought down many influential movers and shakers in Hollywood.

This next close encounter of the lecherous kind will take a little bit of extra explanation. This story began a few months before I got my job at NBC. Picture this: Calabasas, California, when it was a rural, small town with absolutely nothing to do. There were no movie theaters or malls, so going out after dark led most teens to Sambo's diner, which was open twenty-four hours. My friend Julian, a student at Pepperdine University, was on a deadline to finish writing a screenplay for a class. Downing gallons of cheap coffee and devouring stale pastries seemed like the best way to approach this task. It was also the time of a fad that quickly came and went: Mood Rings. These psychedelic stones were made from thermotropic liquid crystals that changed color depending on the body temperature of their wearer. Ostensibly, the green color means you're normal, blue equates to calm, black indicates you're stressed, and dark blue indicates you're happy, romantic, or passionate. I think the word horny was used on the packaging.

Julian and I had a little game we'd play when people entered the restaurant. Since it was such a shitty diner, we'd say things like, "Don't look now, but Elizabeth Taylor came in," or, "It looks like Jack Nicholson ordered a burger to go, and he didn't leave a tip." Anything to break up the monotony as we procrastinated when it came to the writing project. Late into the evening, Julian looked up and said, "Oh look, there's McLean Stevenson." And I said, "Really, what's he doing?" Julian replied, "No, it's really him. Two Highway Patrolmen just carried him in and sat him down at the counter." I turned around, and sure enough, it actually was McLean, best remembered as Lieutenant Colonel Henry Blake from the TV series *M*A*S*H*. It sort of kind of made sense as the exteriors of the TV series were filmed just down the road, but why was he in Sambo's close to midnight?

Upon closer inspection, McLean was perhaps a bit under the influence, and the kindly Highway Patrol officers sat him down and ordered a coffee carafe for him. We eavesdropped as best we could as McLean explained how he'd been a celebrity guest at a golf tournament held down the road. The Highway Patrol officers took McLean's word that he'd sit at the counter for a few hours before getting back in his bright blue Porsche. Julian and I continued working on the screenplay until the subject of my new mood ring came up.

I slipped my mood ring off and handed it to Julian, who waited and watched as the ring's colors changed to reflect his body temperature, I mean, mood. We were laughing and sharing the ring with our waitress, our sweet friend Julie, when McLean turned around and said, "What the hell are you all talking about?" I explained the thermodynamics of this simple piece of costume jewelry as I handed him my ring. Having had numerous cups of coffee by now, McLean immediately registered "Horny" on the less-than-scientifically accurate accessory and began professing his love for me. Seeing this as an opportunity to score...some points, McLean asked if I wanted to go back to his apartment with him. I stood firm, laughing his pass off by saying I would never go to a man's place unless we were married. McLean got down on one knee and proposed. A marriage proposal in Sambo's! It's every girl's dream! Of course, I said yes, because it was all so bizarre. But, how could we get married and go on our honeymoon in the middle of a Sunday night/ Monday morning?

Playing Ethel to my Lucy, waitress Julie and I went into the restroom, and together, we fashioned a wedding dress, veil, and bouquet made from white toilet paper and hand towels. It turned out to be a cute bridal gown, but of course, my groom couldn't see it until everything was in place. At my urging, Julie had two patrons stand with their arms up to make an arch, known as a Chuppah in the Jewish faith. In broken Spanish, Julie asked the fry cook to officiate. He was reluctant, of course. After all, McLean and I had only known each other for a few minutes. Plus, he kept adamantly telling us in broken English that he wasn't a priest. Julie assured him it was all "a broma...a joke."

At last, with Julie as my bridesmaid stoically walking in front of me, I exited the restroom looking like a virginal doily while Julian stood by the side of my soon-to-be husband. McLean used his large gold ring as his wedding band, and I, of course, used my mood ring. There wasn't a dry eye in the house because everyone was laughing so hard. When the ceremony ended, and with the power vested in the short-order cook by Sambo's, I became Mrs. McLean Stevenson. McLean stepped on the Styrofoam coffee cup after the ceremony, the diner erupted in applause, and a few patrons shouted, "Mazel Tov!" Then he gave me a wet, sloppy kiss. He tasted like coffee and cigarettes and something flammable.

Instead of a wedding cake, Julie got a pie for all of us with whipped cream, and we continued our wedding reception, laughing and ignoring the unfinished screenplay. It was late, and McLean once again offered me a tour of his place. There was no way I was going with him. Our faux nuptial would remain unconsummated, but McLean had one more smooth line up his sleeve. McLean leaned in close to me and, in a voice just above a whisper, said, "I'm hosting *The Tonight Show* tomorrow night. Would you like to be my guest?" "I'd love to go!" shrieked Julian. Then Julie started clapping her hands, saying she wanted to go. It looked like my hubby, the host, would have three guests watching from the VIP seats. Could his suave move have backfired any worse? We went to the show and afterward said a brief hello to my soon-to-be ex-husband, thanking him for the tickets and telling him how much fun we had. That was the last I saw of him until I got my job at NBC.

McLean was now the darling of NBC. His character on *M*A*S*H* had been killed off, and he was free to continue guest-hosting *The Tonight Show*. He even began taping his self-titled sitcom, *The McLean Stevenson Show in* Studio 4. McLean played Mac, a husband looking forward to living at home with his loving wife, Peggy (played by Barbara Stuart), in peace and quiet until his divorced children and grandchildren all move in with them. And, oh yes, Peggy's mom comes to live with them, too.

I would sit in the dark in the back row of the bleachers in Studio 4, absorbing everything I could during the rehearsals and taping. I wanted to learn about the characters and watch the writers rewrite on the spot. Basically, I was learning everything about the format, characters, and pacing of the script until I could come up with a story to pitch to McLean, maybe even a spec script showing him how hilarious I could be on his sitcom staff. I saw this as my way onto the writing staff of a network show.

I knew the show had a pedigree of established, knowledgeable comedy writers, but perhaps in Season Two I too, could get a staff writing job, or they could throw me a script to write. This is how a twenty-one-year-old thinks when she thinks she knows everything.

With the now totally passé mood ring firmly tucked in the pocket of my Page blazer, I gave tours of the hallways in Burbank until one day I spotted McLean. He would usually provide a cursory wave to the tour group and keep moving. On this occasion, I put the mood ring on my finger and introduced McLean to the crowd, forcing him to stand still for a moment to acknowledge the group and me. I made several hand gestures prominently featuring the wedding mood ring. It took a moment for it to dawn on him what I was doing, what I was wearing, and who I was. Yep, he remembered what happened that night. I didn't think he was glad to see me, but I guess he was because of what happened a few days later.

A small section of the second floor in the main building across from Studio 4 was dedicated to the Guest Relations phone lines and the ticket distribution office. When we weren't giving tours or ushering shows, we were supposed to open fan mail, stuff envelopes with tickets, man the phone lines, give people directions to the facility, answer questions, record complaints or compliments on NBC's programming, and, in some cases, field death threats. The network gave McLean an office next to Guest Relations, which must have been distracting and with all the phones ringing and people traipsing in and out throughout the day.

McLean must have seen me go into the Guest Relations office and asked one of the Pages to tell me he wanted to see me. What is the old expression about luck? It's when experience meets opportunity, and this was about to be my big break! I had some story ideas for his show, typed and ready to go. I took the paper out of my purse, neatly folded it, and put it in my pocket. I combed my hair, put on lipstick, and tried to look as professional as a gal could look in polyester. In my mind, I was already dusting off a place on my nonexistent mantel for my Emmy and remembering to be sure to thank McLean in my speech.

I knocked on his door, and McLean greeted me with a big smile. He invited me into his office. There was a large desk, lots of correspondence, scripts, and trade papers. The furniture wasn't new, but the lamps matched. There weren't any posters or plaques with his present or past accomplishments lining the walls. It was fairly spartan. We exchanged pleasantries, laughing over how we'd first met and married. I told him I had our marriage annulled at Taco Bell, and that got a laugh. I found my moment to say how I had studied his show and that I had a few ideas for future scripts. I took the paper from my pocket and handed it to McLean.

The one thing I couldn't have noticed when I entered his office was the secret button under the middle desk drawer. Without warning, the door to McLean's office suddenly slammed closed. He gave me "The Look." You know, the "Hey baby, what say we test out the cushions on the couch look." I was in shock! Did he think I wanted...was he trying to... what was happening? And then I was in hysterics, laughing, I mean laughing really, really hard, trying to catch my breath. Gasping, I looked at McLean, pointing at him, saying, "You don't understand. This is all out of some Doris Day movie. You're the masher, and you were on *M*A*S*H*, and you were on *The Doris Day Show*, and this is so surreal!" I continued to point and laugh uncontrollably. You'd think that would be enough of a boner killer, but no.

McLean stood up from behind the desk and began walking. I assumed he would open the door so that I could leave, but instead, he lunged toward me, knocking me back onto the couch, pressing himself against me, and began forcibly holding me down. This was getting all too real. I don't know how I did what I did next. He was scaring me, and I had to do something to scare him. The words just flowed out of my mouth with all the experience and authority I didn't have. "Listen, we can do this, and trust me, I would be the best lay you ever had. But, I'm due at *The Tonight Show* in ten minutes, and when I'm late, and someone asks me why I was late, and sweaty, I'll tell them I was upstairs getting nasty with McLean Stevenson. Or, you can get off me right now, and we'll never speak of this again." He paused a moment. At this point, I suspect both our careers were flashing before our eyes. In what felt like an eternity, he let go of my wrists and climbed off me, opening the door, never saying a word.

I calmly walked out the door and, when I was out of his line of sight, hurried down the stairs and ran into the ladies' room for a moment of solitude. I was trembling and began hyperventilating. I kept asking myself, "What did I do wrong? I thought I'd made it abundantly clear that I was only after a writing job, not him. How could I be so stupid?" My inner monologue turned to self-doubt, "Who are you kidding? You'll never be a writer. Men will only ever look at you like a piece of ass, not a professional. You should have known better. Why even bother to have a dream if it can be crushed so easily?"

My colleagues at *The Tonight Show* could tell I was shook-up about something. The Page Supervisor pulled me aside, and without going into too many details, I said McLean had put some serious moves on me. The Supervisor told me, and I'll never forget this, "Ahh, he's done that to other girls on the Page staff, too. He even followed Sandy Petersen down to the Page lounge."

So now, on top of all of this, I wasn't even somehow "special" to him. I had so many conflicted feelings, including being jealous of the other women he'd hit on. I know, crazy, right? The mid-seventies was still the era of "boys will be boys," so I never reported the incident. Who would have believed a lowly Page over TV's McLean Stevenson? It took me too much time and many talks with my friends, male and female to stop blaming myself for what happened. As a child of divorce, I could have been a poster child for trust issues. It's not like we met at a hotel or someplace off the NBC lot. It was in a professional environment. What started as something fun with us, laughing about the past, soon became uncomfortable and threatening. Despite my clear intention for agreeing to meet, everything he did: manipulation, his closing the door via a concealed button, and the pounce were all orchestrated before I even set foot in his office. Emotionally, this set me back in ways I only realized once women and men came forward with their stories of similar encounters during the inception of the #MeToo movement. In many companies, the Human Resources Department has set guidelines for inappropriate speech or actions in the workplace. Intimidation should not be a limitation when it comes to protecting yourself and your coworkers in reporting people who violate these terms of employment. Yes, it is easier said than done, but do it. Say something and let the world know who the people are that are ready to take advantage of our kindness and earnestness to achieve.

Chapter Twelve

MIDNIGHT SPECIAL, PRYOR & THE POLICE

Friday night, following *The Tonight Show, The Midnight Special* shined its ever-lovin' light on an eclectic mix of rock, country, blues, and disco singers, along with performances by comics including George Carlin, Steve Martin, and Andy Kaufman. For the first season, singer Helen Reddy hosted the show, then the gravely voiced, over-the-top radio legend Wolfman Jack took over the reins. And yes, the opening credits were sung by the man that made the song *The Midnight Special* famous, Johnny Rivers.

When the show aired, it looked and sounded like a seamless concert. That wasn't how it was at all. The show was a giant patchwork of pretaped musical acts and comics all dropped into different episodes throughout the season. The audience sat on the floor for hours, sometimes on pillows, watching the bands sing, mostly live, the same song two or three times to get it just right. It was refreshing to see and hear live music. Sometimes, that's all the audience would see. Other times, the band might do two or three different songs, and there might be a comic to keep them entertained between setups. Not all the acts were a big draw. Some singers didn't appeal to an older crowd, and it could be challenging to get an audience. Sitting on the floor for hours didn't help. I remember going over to the Mexican restaurant across the street, trying in vain to recruit people to see The Bee Gees. I had a few takers. A year later, the film *Saturday Night Fever* was released, featuring the pulsating beat and lyrics of *"Stayin' Alive"*, and the heartfelt harmonies of *"How Deep Is Your Love"*. The rest is music history.

If you were assigned to work the show, you pretty much planned on staying late because musicians didn't always arrive at their appointed call time. And when they left, there were often empty vodka or Jack Daniel's bottles in the trash cans. Very occasionally, you could catch a whiff of weed wafting through the hallway.

Marilee Mahoney remembers the afternoon when she let her inner rock and roll fantasy freak flag fly. Disco sensation Gloria Gaynor was late for her lighting and camera-blocking rehearsal. As the track of her hit song, *"I Will Survive,"* blasted through the speakers, the director attempted to position the camera and design the lighting to match the moves Gloria might make. But then, who jumped onto the stage but Marilee, lip-sinking and gyrating to the beat! Her moment in the spotlight didn't last long as the director, his booming voice reverberating over the loudspeakers, yelled, "Cut! Cut! Cut! Marilee, get off the stage!"

I saw so many performers I could never afford to see at concert venues: Elton John, Billy Joel, Aerosmith, Diana Ross, The Village People, and The Jackson 5. One of the Page perks is that we could sneak our friends into the shows, too!

While working *Midnight Special,* Courtney found himself face-to-face with Helen Reddy's husband, Jeff Wald. He was one of the most prominent personal managers in town, with a roster of A-list stars from the film, television, and music world. Jeff learned the hard way that you should be nice to people on the way up because you never know where you'll run into them again. As Courtney recalled, with a chuckle in his voice, "He wanted me to leave my CB spot to pick up a package for him at the front gate. I said, 'I can't leave my post.' He said, 'Why the fuck can't you do that?' and he started screaming at me, and he was this big (indicating short in stature), and I said, 'I can't do it,' and he started to throw a phone at me. It came back because it was attached to the wall. Then I said, 'That wasn't very cool, Mr. Reddy.' That just made him madder.

My father, Gino Conte, who was Director of Production Services, and his colleagues, Bob Corwin and Dick Wendelkin, the group of guys that ran the place, were walking by, and I said, 'This guy just threw a phone at me, and he told me I was fired.' And then, Bob Corwin had him escorted off the lot. Flash ahead, I'm at Carsey-Werner, and Roseanne (Barr) has a new manager, and when I saw him said, 'Do you remember me?'

He said, "No."

I said, 'We had a little altercation at *Midnight Special* when I wouldn't pick up lunch for you, and you threw a phone at me?'

Jeff said, "I was so coked out of my brain then, and I had no idea what I was doing, and I apologize." And then we had a great fucking time laughing about how crazy people are."

But one group, one night, stands out above all others. It has become known as "The Midnight Massacre." It was a Scottish invasion, The Bay City Rollers, billed as the "Tartan Teen Sensations from Edinburgh." We had never heard of them but were told they were the next big thing to cross the pond since The Beatles.

The Pages assigned to the show were utterly unprepared. They were outnumbered by screaming teenagers carrying signs with the names of their favorite band members; Les, Derek, and Eric waving an inordinate amount of various tartan fabrics in the air.

The band's name was spelled out in gigantic red light bulbs several stories high. When it was illuminated, the screaming fans went wild! When The Bay City Rollers took the stage, a sea of teens raced forward to be near their idols. The fans couldn't get enough of their tartan-trimmed jumpsuits or of a hairless-chested Les McKeown as he belted out the first song, "*Saturday Night.*"

Jim McDonald, sensing this was a dangerous situation, put out an APB (All Page Bulletin). The Pages working *The Tonight Show* were told to head over to Studio 2 at the end of their shift to help control the crowd. The fans had turned into fanatics! They were too close to the stage, touching members of the band as they played. The Pages working the show had been given a rope to hold back the crowd, but the fans were trampling them. As the crowd moved closer and closer, it became a dangerous situation.

The stage started shifting. Girls were pulling Dinah Brein's hair, and someone slugged her in the face, giving her a black eye. Michael Borison punched the girl back and then threw her out of the studio. The Pages begged Jim to have the control room order the teens to step back from the stage, but they refused. Brian Robinette remembers, "It was (Dinah) that made me order the Pages to drop the rope and get out from between the teenyboppers and the stage that Tuesday night. When I saw (her) eyes popping out from all the pressing girls, I knew that we were done being the show's security guards that night." Lesa recalled the events saying, "Chris Gallagher was my hero that night. I remember her telling me, 'We're not security guards' and to get out of there." I tried to help, but Jim threw himself against the door of the stage and, with his arms outstretched, yelled, "Don't go in there! You'll get killed."

The next day, as Brian recalled, Jay Michelis held a meeting of all the Pages who worked the show. Also present in the private viewing room were Hank Rieger from the Publicity Department and the head of NBC security. They explained to Jay exactly what had happened. Brian went on to say, "I remember that meeting well. Ambulances were called. They weren't happy we sent all those kids to St. Joseph's (Hospital). Jay was furious with the producers and defended the Pages for trying to hold their positions."

I always suspected someone associated with promoting The Bay City Rollers wanted a moment like The Beatles had when they appeared on *The Ed Sullivan Show*. We've all seen the iconic black and white footage of the girls screaming and crying when The Beatles sang their first song, *"All My Loving,"* that magical night on February 9, 1964. The Bay City Rollers crowd looked like an orchestrated publicity stunt, and the Pages got caught in the middle of the mayhem. Then again, I suppose hundreds of girls could show up carrying the exact same signs and reams of the same plaid fabric? Unfortunately, that wasn't the only time Pages had to deal with an unruly audience.

It was 1977. NBC proudly proclaimed they had Pryor, Richard Pryor. He was the stand-up's stand-up, revered for his jokes as much as the characters he created. He was primarily known to mainstream audiences as a film star in *Lady Sings the Blues*, as the Piano Man, and from his starring roles in iconic comedies including *Car Wash* and *Silver Streak*. Pryor was also a writer on the film *Blazing Saddles*, where his uncensored dialogue was not only welcome, it was encouraged.

There was trouble from the first day, or should I say night, of taping. According to the Outside Page in Charge (OIC), Tom Hansen, the show may not have gone on at all if it weren't for Pryor's close friend, writer Paul Moody. "Paul was a gentle, soft-spoken man who tried to do his best to appease the guy who was paying him," Hansen said. "People had begun arriving early for a 5:00 taping. The line wrapped around the block, and Paul had to tell the crowd that they would be starting a little late. The Pages reported that Pryor was drugged or stoned or both, and he wouldn't come out of his dressing room to rehearse, but Moody, protecting his friend, told the crowd, 'Richard was under the weather.' Moody came back a total of three times to appease the growing crowd. Then, there were other problems. Pryor demanded the first two rows of seats be filled with only Black ticket holders. Hansen looked at the line, which white people primarily populated, and told Moody, "There are people who have been standing here for over four hours. The first 40 people in line were all white. Paul, this is going to be a problem." Tom said Moody was resourceful and decided to go to the back of the extremely long line, discreetly ushering couples and groups of Black guests into the audience. But when Hansen was able to let the audience in, there was another problem. There was an overflow crowd, and, it turns out, Pryor wouldn't be taping an entire show that night, only two sketches. To avoid an inevitable riot, Tom was instructed by the production company to let everyone in, a direct violation of the rules set by the fire marshal.

The first sketch, which didn't start taping until 11:00 p.m., six hours late, was a send-up on the famous *Star Wars* bar scene. The crowd, sitting in the aisles of the bleachers, blocking the walkways to the exits, were more than ready to see Pryor, who played a bartender serving drinks to an array of *Star Wars* creatures. There was a script, but that didn't stop Pryor from ad-libbing a lot of the dialogue, including the "N" word. The clip I viewed online did not censor the word, but I don't know if it made it on the air. At the beginning of the sketch, you can hear genuine audience laughter, but as the scene progresses, it becomes apparent the laughter had been sweetened by editors who added extra laughs and applause.

That's because, as witnesses could attest, the sketch was horrible and dragged on and on. A second sketch didn't begin taping until 2:00 a.m. By now, most of the audience was gone, and the Pages were getting double-overtime pay.

After a few hours of sleep, Tom and the Pages who worked the Pryor show were summoned to Eba's office. Eba wanted to know exactly what happened in Studio 2 and why it happened the way it did. Also in the room were members of the Burbank Police Department and NBC lawyers. Hansen was concerned about why NBC had to defend itself. "I guess they were trying to get their ducks in a row. How concerned were all these people about what happened last night." Tom learned that Pryor had a clause in his contract stating his company could distribute tickets to the taping. Given the size of the crowd, Tom said, "They must have flown over LA dropping tickets from a helicopter." Tom told me he requested not to work on the show again, which turned out to be okay because the Pryor show executives demanded that only Black Pages work the show in the future.

The show was canceled after four episodes. Pryor had well-documented battles with the NBC censors. Still, he was ultimately a victim of low ratings and the realization that, under the circumstances, he couldn't deliver a quality variety show week after week.

Chapter Thirteen

A SIDE OF FRIES

Workplace romances were nothing new, but two middle-management employees took their affair to a whole new level. Their affair was one of the worst-kept secrets and has become legendary. He was married. She was, too, until her husband was found dead when she came home from work. There was no sign of foul play or suicide. We heard it could have been an aneurysm, but none of us knew definitively. Shortly after the widow returned to work, she decided to redecorate her office with, of all things, a couch she brought from home, the same couch on which her husband took his last breath. I would be asked to come into her office and have a seat, but I never sat on that couch. It was too creepy to think about the sofa's history and even creepier to know that she and her lover were still using the couch for a bit of afternoon delight.

A few relationships were genuine, and they survived the challenges of being a married couple who both have successful careers in the entertainment industry. Renee Palyo became a writer/producer on shows, including *Saved By the Bell*, while her husband, Tim Jones, was an actor and stand-up comic. Tim's work often took him away from home, but Renee and their son, Blake, could occasionally join him while touring beautiful locations around the world. To the best of my knowledge, Blake is the only child I know of to have former Pages as parents.

I had always heard the expression you shouldn't date people you work with, but I couldn't help it when I became a little fascinated by this guy about ten years older than me. His name was Travis, and he worked in a different division of Guest Relations. I would see him daily, and we exchanged pleasantries. He seemed like a terrific guy, and he checked off many of the boxes in my brain as to what would be good causal boyfriend material. He wasn't too tall, he was ruggedly handsome and athletic, took exotic vacations, raced cars, and had romanced a few of the women on the staff. All reports were he was a nice guy who wasn't ready to settle down. Perfect. No way he'd get in the way of my career goals.

I feigned interest in something he was talking about, and a few days later, he asked me to join him and "The Boys" for dinner at DuPars, the best place in town to get a slice of pie. They were a fun group of guys, successful in their various eclectic jobs. They were the kind of guys who knew a guy who knew a guy that could fix anything or get you anything you needed. And, refreshingly, they never talked down about women. Come to think of it they really didn't talk about women at all. Mostly about cars. Cars and basketball. Cars, basketball, and skiing. And the old days. Lots of talk about the old days. They laughed a lot and razzed each other, and constantly tried to figure out which one of them was a bigger knucklehead.

Later that evening, Travis asked me to come back to his home just south of Ventura Boulevard in Studio City. I agreed but insisted I drive myself to his house so I could leave if I didn't feel comfortable. I need not have worried as he immediately made me feel welcome. He handed me a drink, then kissed me gently on the cheek. He showed me around the house, but we never got to the bedroom. We kissed intensely, my lower back pressed against the knob of the bathroom door. I didn't want this moment to end, so I slowly started bending my knees as I lowered us to the carpeted floor of the hallway. Still entwined in a lip-lock, his rough manly hands slowly removed my panties, and he, with ballet grace and control, positioned himself to my side, touching, groping, tantalizing my body, removing what remained of my clothing. Oh, he had done this before. I silently thanked the women he had known before me on whom he'd practiced this technique. I somehow managed to find my blouse and laid it on the carpet so as not to get rug burn, and we proceeded to make love in every position a narrow hallway could accommodate. Damn, it was fun and satisfying, and did I say satisfying?

Days later, I drove directly from work to Travis' house. He had the barbecue going, with two steaks sizzling on the grill that had been marinating all day. Hell, I had been marinating all day in anticipation of another night of passion and pleasure. We set the table, and he poured the wine as we made small talk. He asked me to taste the salad dressing, an old family recipe, then kissed me on the neck. Dinner was served, and to my surprise, he was an excellent cook. We talked about his adventures and how he would like to travel with someone, but he'd had a hard time meeting a woman who could pick up and go at a moment's notice. Did he even know how fabulous he was? I excused myself to freshen up, and when I returned, Travis had cleared the table and stacked the dishes in the dishwasher. Did I stumble into a relationship without ever knowing or wanting one?

We adjourned to the living room rug and started rolling around like a couple of frisky teens who had the whole house to themselves, giggling and groping. What was it about the floor that he liked? It didn't matter because we could have been on a bed of nails, and it would have been perfect. Just as the clothes were coming off, "The Boys" burst through the front door and plopped themselves on the couch, seemingly oblivious to our precoital hanky-panky. I quickly fumbled to button my blouse while Travis greeted his visitors, leaving me on the floor. He excused himself from the guys, picked me up, threw me over his shoulder, and shouted back to the fellas, "Put the game on. I won't be too long. Oh, and you remember Shelley."

He threw me down on his bed (at least I now knew he had a bed) and quickly started unbuckling his pants. I sat up and said, "Slow down, Cowboy. What just happened?" Travis told me these are his "Boys" and that they are always welcome at his place, day or night. Now, I'm not one of those people who give ultimatums, but I did ask if, in the future, he could tell "The Boys" they should call first in case I was at his place. Travis agreed, but the thrill was gone, and we didn't have the hot sex I'd hoped for that night. I told him he could wait in the bedroom awhile so his buddies would think he was getting busy with me, but he left, asking for a rain check to make it up to me. I said goodnight to "The Boys" and slunk out of the house like some backstreet trollop.

Third night. Makeup sex was on the menu, and I was more than willing to partake in the feast. I watched the clock on the wall all day until it was quitting time. Yabba Dabba Doo! I changed out of my Page uniform and put on a casual, yet sexy, accessible little outfit. I stopped by the liquor store on the corner of his street to buy some chilled Champagne, a peace offering, and a classy prelude to the romance that awaited.

Travis took the plate of hors d'oeuvres he had prepared and placed them on the coffee table. We sat down, sipping our drinks, unwinding from the day. I put my head on his shoulder, and he played with my hair. It felt good. It felt right. A career gal like myself could get used to this.

Without warning, the front door burst open. The "Boys" were back in town. They headed straight for the couch, grabbing the hors d'oeuvers as they sat down, propping their feet on the coffee table. A night of romance? What could I have been thinking? The Lakers were playing, and for some reason, it was somehow crucial they all watch it together, like they always did, at Travis' place.

Travis' attention immediately shifted from me to what was on the TV, his energy now consumed by the testosterone-filled guests in the room. I gave Travis a "what the hell" look, and he just shrugged and smiled. He then pulled $20 out of his wallet and asked if I could go over to McDonald's and get "The Boys" something to eat. Oh, I would get the "Boys" something to eat. I was furious Travis didn't think our relationship, friendship, fuck-buddieship, whatever we were in was more important than "The Boys." We were officially done, over, and worst of all, we had to see each other at work every day. But what to do? What to do? A moment of inspiration came to me when I looked at the McDonald's menu. Keep in mind; this was 1977 money. I bought $20 worth of french fries. Just french fries. I could barely carry them back to Travis' house, but I gained strength with each step I took, playing Wagner's "The Ride of The Valkyries" in my head. I slowly opened the unlocked front door and quietly slipped into the living room. The TV was blaring, and "The Boys" had no idea I was in the room. I quietly opened the numerous bags of fries, then walked behind the couch, dumping all the fries on the guys. To say they were pissed was an understatement. I walked around to the front of the coffee table, grabbed what was left of the champagne with one hand, then pointed my finger at Travis and told him never to call me again. Travis just sat there as though he'd never seen a woman stand up for herself. And yes, I slammed the door when I left.

Meanwhile, back at the studio, I dreaded seeing Travis again. I made a concerted effort to stay away from his office, taking the longer route around the hallways, burying myself in my tour groups in the hope he wouldn't see me. Leave it to me to make a cringe-worthy situation even cringier. Don't get me wrong. I was damn proud I stood up for myself. I just didn't think about the big picture, or if I did, I thought I could skate through any side-eye glances or office gossip. In what seemed like an eternity (but was only three days in scorned lover time,) I saw Travis, walking alone from the commissary, chomping on an apple, still looking sexy as hell. He saw I saw him. Damn, no escape. I took a deep breath, held my head high, and continued at a confident pace toward him, buttoning my jacket. As I approached him, he stopped, put his hand in his pocket, and said, "You left these at my house." In his hand were a pair of silver hoop earrings. I smiled, looked him in the eyes, and calmly said, "They aren't mine," and I was on my way. But that wasn't the last time I saw Travis.

Several decades later, I got a call. The voice was mistakable. He said, "Can you guess who this is?" Hell, if I knew. Drawing on my game show question writing background and not wanting to appear totally ignorant, I said, "Let's play 20 Questions." For some reason, the first question I asked, thinking I was being disarming and humorous was, "Did we ever have sex?" There was a long pause, and Travis said, "I think so." I think so? I think so? He identified himself and told me our mutual friend, Brian Robinette, gave him my number. Brian had no idea of our history, but still, Brian shouldn't have given out my number. Travis told me he was married, had two sons, and had an idea for a television show. Out of intense curiosity, I agreed to meet with him at Art's Deli, where I could show up looking fabulous. I got there exactly on time, expecting to make a grand entrance when Travis pulled up to the front of the restaurant riding a Harley. He parked the bike, took off his helmet, bounded to the entrance and gave me a big hug. Yeah, he still had it going on, and his charisma level was an eleven.

We ate, superficially reminisced, laughed, and he told me his idea for a TV show. It was a good idea, and we worked together for about six months. It wasn't until our last meeting with the network, when the idea was ultimately rejected, that I summoned the courage to asked if he remembered why we stopped speaking to each other. He cocked his head to the side and smiled his megawatt smile. He was clueless. I explained the whole story: The Floor, The Boys, The French Fries. He looked at me like I was from outer space. He had no earthly idea what I was talking about, then shrugged. My grand gesture, the story I've dined on for decades, only merited a shrug?

I've told the story of The French Fries Guy to friends over the years. And each time, I get the same reaction. Most of the men think I was a bitch, and all of the women say, "Way to go!" When I told my husband the french fries part of this story, he asked if I got ketchup for the fries. That's just one of the reasons I married him.

Chapter Fourteen

WHAT NOT TO DO

I secured an internship with Ralph Andrews Production (RAP) for the last two semesters of my less-than-illustrious college career. His company produced the game shows *You Don't Say, Celebrity Sweepstakes,* and *50 Grand Slam* for NBC. Ralph's company was also in production with a syndicated revival of a show he first created in 1969, *Liar's Club,* hosted by Rod Serling. Yeah, the creator of *The Twilight Zone* hosted a game show.

Ralph was a character unto himself. He looked like Mister Clean, with a clean-shaven head, minus the earring. Ralph was loud and boisterous and charismatic and often carried a gun on his person. Little did I know how easy it was to get an internship with his company because Ralph became notorious for not paying his employees, contestants, or the line of creditors around the block. Before I began my stint learning the inner workings of the game show biz, Ralph had gathered staff to tell them the weekly paychecks were going to be late. Later that same day, he pulled into his parking space in his new gold Rolls Royce. Ralph said that image was everything and wanted the buyers of his shows to think rumors of his insolvency had been greatly exaggerated.

There were other financial bumps in the road. On one occasion, I noticed the gold coins that had been embedded into the sides of Ralph's magnificent mahogany pool table had been removed with what looked like scratches made by a dull kitchen knife and replaced with tarnished silver dollars. In the lunchroom at most production companies, the cabinets were filled with snacks for the taking and there was a refrigerator stocked with water and sodas. Instead, Ralph had "Honor Snacks," a selection of candy bars and potato chips, in a cardboard box with a slot on the side where we could pay for our treats. I guess Ralph used the change for gas money. The irony of having anything "honorable" associated with Ralph never escapes me.

Ralph was always coming up with ideas for game shows, and we'd have fun preparing run-throughs to show network honchos what could be the next big game show blockbuster. I learned to build sets, write questions, and see how the bones of a new show are assembled. It was like tuning a car to each buyer's specifications. Should it be an easy show, a personality-driven format, or just a straight-up question-and-answer format? We'd have fun asking friends to play the game, testing material, and scoring to see what worked best. If Ralph found a potential buyer, even if the game wasn't quite 100 percent yet, in true Ralph fashion, we'd rig the run-throughs in the hopes of getting a development deal. I thought this man was a genius, and witnessing him in action was better training than any Master's Degree I could have earned at Cal State Northridge.

Ralph's shenanigans didn't end there. While taping *Celebrity Sweepstakes,* a show that depended on the studio audience voting on which celebrity would answer a question correctly, Ralph would run through the aisle, frantically pressing the buttons in front of empty seats, randomly setting the odds on how the voting would be calculated. This was a big game show no-no. Why? Because it wasn't an honest reading of the odds from those members who were actually voting in the studio audience. The Broadcast Standards department told Ralph several times not to do this, but he did it anyway. On the few days I worked on the show, Ralph, often dressed in a matching patchwork denim jacket and pants, was not allowed in the studio during the taping of his own show.

Looking to expand his empire from game shows to big-time event specials, Ralph made a somewhat shady deal with Evel Knievel, best remembered for his two historical television moments. One, his 1967 stunt of jumping, then crashing his motorcycle over the fountain at Caesars Palace in Las Vegas, and two, his ill-fated attempt to cross a section of Idaho's Snake River in a rocket-powered cycle, only to crash on the banks of the river, narrowly escaping death. Evel's newest idea was to do a stunt that involved jumping out of an airplane without a parachute or net. I believe he believed he could do it. Perhaps the contents of the decorative Wild Turkey decanter Evel was liberally swigging from that gave him the liquid courage to try to sell it as a show. And, in a stroke of genius that PT Barnum would envy, Ralph came up with an idea to add a gambling element to the event. Since Evel had to land on something soft, why not put twelve haystacks on the ground, and let people wager on which haystack Evel would land? And, if it were the haystack with the special needle, the bettor would win more. Ralph even tried to find a country that would allow such betting, including wagering if Evel would survive the stunt. There were no takers. Ralph never saw the multitude of problems associated with these ideas. Ultimately, it was a way to lure unsuspecting backers into funding the project, knowing full well that the FAA would never authorize such a jump in the US. But stranger shows have been produced.

I couldn't wait to change out of my Page uniform to hang out at the RAP offices for a minimum of twelve hours a week. It was a bastion of creativity led by former *Hogan's Heroes* star Larry Hovis. Larry was the Executive Producer of *Liar's Club* and had somehow managed to recruit (and keep) a loyal group of people who worked long hours to find the unusual items or artwork that could be used on the show. Here's how *Liar's Club* was played: four celebrity panelists each told two contestants a story as to what the strange item could be. The contestant who picked the correct item got points, and the person with the most points won. It wasn't a lot of cash, but they had a lot of fun.

There were a few secrets to making this format work. First was, we never, I emphasize, never, ever, told the host, venerable game show icon, Allen Ludden, what the item was before the announcer revealed it. If Allen stopped by the office on a non-tape day, we'd all scurry to cover the items with black cloths so he couldn't get a peek at the crazy contraptions and unintentionally spill the beans when we were taping. Second, we flat-out lied to the celebrity panelists. That was Larry's inspired idea. If the celebrity thought they had the correct story, they could sell it better, making their story all the more believable.

The series attracted some big stars who were fans of the format, including Charlton Heston and Burt Reynolds. Before becoming a late-night legend, David Letterman guested a few times. So did Allen's wife, Betty White. When Betty guested on the panel, she'd arrive with her mother, Tess. It was so sweet to see them together. Tess told me that on the days Betty taped *Liar's Club,* the two would spend the morning at the Elizabeth Arden Salon in Beverly Hills to get their hair and nails done. Tess would get her hair curled and teased like Betty's hairdo, and the manicurist made sure the mother and daughter duo continued their twinning by having their fingernails filed and polished to look identical by sharing the same shade.

Larry played an elaborate practical joke on Betty that nearly backfired big time. Knowing Betty had friends, both animal and human, at the LA Zoo, Larry began telling her a story about some strange animal noises he'd been hearing behind his home. A few weeks later, when she appeared on *Liar's Club* again, he said he saw strange footprints in his backyard. This got Betty's attention. She asked Larry if he could somehow document what he'd seen. So, Larry made a giant paw print in his backyard, poured plaster into it, and presented the "evidence" to Betty. Larry didn't anticipate how fascinated Betty would become with the plaster paw print. She went to her dressing room, called the LA Zoo, and asked if someone could come to the studio to see Larry's discovery. Larry had to pump the brakes on the joke and finally told Betty the truth. At first, she was a bit upset, but not because the joke was played on her. She was more disappointed that Larry hadn't discovered Bigfoot.

Larry was also a soft touch for lesser-known actors, comics, and show biz friends who had fallen on hard times, who often asked to be booked on the show simply to earn enough money to qualify for union medical insurance.

As part of my internship, I would be on the lookout for doodads Larry might consider for the show. Viewers were encouraged to send items they wanted to see on the show, and we had our own team of tchotchke experts: Jimmy, Gregg, Big Bob, and Laurie, AKA "Bumpers," a true pinball wizard who honed her skills on the Evel Knievel pinball machine gifted to Ralph by the daredevil himself.

We would look through catalogs, scour antique stores, and search medical and restaurant supply houses. Part of our job was to make sure we had two independent sources verifying the correct story about the item or artwork. After all, the show was called *Liar's Club,* and three of the lies also had to be completely different from the correct answer, leaving no doubt as to what story was the only correct answer.

When possible, we would back up our story by citing the item's patent or provenance. But when someone sends a rolled piece of cloth that looks like a cigarette and tells you his grandpa used to stick items like this in his ear, and light it on fire to remove earwax, well, you just have to go with it!

Once, Larry asked me to join him at comic Buddy Hackett's home in Beverly Hills to look at some items for the show. The landmark home was on a corner lot facing Whittier Drive and was famous for the large cement elephant near the front entrance. Buddy showed us his collection of guns. Larry was fascinated, but I started getting anxious. I was afraid to get near them, even when Buddy showed me they were empty before handing them over to Larry.

Two things stuck in my mind about his home. One: he had two kitchens, one of traditional means and the other for Kosher meals. Two: there was a beauty salon chair with a hairdryer placed against the wall of weapons. It was uniquely out of place in his beautifully furnished home. He explained to us it was Johnny Carson's chair. Johnny was the only guest Buddy would allow to smoke cigarettes in his home, with the provision he'd have to sit in the salon chair, so the smoke could be exhausted through the dryer apparatus.

Allen invited the *Liar's Club* gang to a taping of a pilot for a sitcom, eponymously titled, *The Betty White Show.* Betty played an actress who discovers, much to her horror, that her ex-husband is the director of the series. Allen was excited and nervous for her and was a bit antsy that evening. He didn't want to remain seated. I joined him at the back of the studio, where he stood with his arms crossed, beaming at Betty. He turned to me and said, "Isn't she marvelous!" I love hearing husbands speak highly of their wives.

Once a week, we'd gather in Larry's extremely cluttered office to go over the items we'd discovered. Each of us would hold the items and tell a story, explaining what it could be. It was a fun way to get the lies, the wrong story about the object. Larry would write the ideas on index cards he placed on a bulletin board wall, arranging and rearranging the cards to get enough variety for five shows a day that were taped. I so looked forward to these brainstorming sessions because the people in the room were so intelligent and funny. If they liked one of my ideas, I felt like part of the team. It was a nurturing, free-wheeling, hysterically funny environment that, thankfully, Ralph had little to do with.

It's not to say we didn't do a few semi-shady things along the way. Christmas Eve, 1977, I received a call at home from Larry. He had heard on the radio that a family was in desperate need. A widower, diagnosed with a fatal brain tumor, had just been released from the hospital. He didn't have time to get his two small children food or presents for what would be their last Christmas together. Larry asked if I had any unopened Christmas presents lying around my house. I was just about to crack into a five-pound box of See's Candies when he asked that I meet him at the office as soon as possible. I re-wrapped the candy and brought along a few small gifts I'd received but hadn't used. The whole gang was also there, with flour, sugar, eggs, milk, and anything that could be purchased at 7-11 convenience store on Christmas Eve. Larry had the key to the office's front door but not the key to the prize room. Ralph kept many prizes for himself that should have been sent to contestants on his various shows. So, with a screwdriver, a hammer, and a credit card, we proceeded to break into the room and grab a load of loot (along with some lovely Mary Kay Cosmetics). I felt like Larry was Robin Hood, and we were the Merry Men robbing from the rich and giving to the poor. Through his game show connections, Larry even arranged to have a new washer and dryer sent to the family.

We were a close-knit group, even traveling to Las Vegas to compete in a charity inner-tube racing event. But one field trip stands out in my mind. The image is burned into a part of my brain where it can never be erased. Larry received a videotape in the mail of items from Europe to possibly use on the show. The tape was in a PAL format (Phase Alternating Line), the standard in Europe, and we were unable to play on any VHS or Beta video machines used in the United States. Larry called a producer friend of his who had just such a PAL machine in his office. We grabbed our notepads, made a couple of peanut butter and jelly sandwiches, and took the tape to an upscale building in Beverly Hills. The receptionist let us into a magnificent suite with a wet bar and plush sofas. The walls were lined with photos of famous people and numerous awards. The suite even had a private bathroom and shower. It was a sharp contrast from the spartan conditions at Ralph's office.

The producer's office entertainment center resembled Mission Control. Larry began pushing many buttons, attempting to figure out which machine was which and how to play the tape. While I was admiring the ocean view, I suddenly heard moaning sounds, then a sloshing sound. Larry had accidentally turned on one of the numerous VCR machines, and when I looked over there he was: the producer, the guy in all the pictures on the wall, was also on the screen. He was naked, lying on his back on a waterbed, fully erect (and uncircumcised,) with a very famous, very blonde woman going down on him. The blonde was trying her best to please the guy with her mouth and nimble hands. He paid little attention to her flawless body. Instead, he concentrated on how he looked in the monitor, adjusting his position to an angle that would show off his manliness, tilting the blonde's head and finding the right angle for the money shot. It wasn't romantic or hot at all. It was kind of pathetic. And I watched every frame!

We never did watch the PAL tape from Europe. Larry was good friends with the woman on the tape and knew it would be disastrous for her if the video were ever leaked. So, Larry stole the tape. We went directly back to the office and cut the tape into pieces, setting the magnetic bits on fire in the parking lot. I never mentioned it again to Larry until 2003, a few days before he died, telling him how much I respected him for destroying the tape.

Larry was interested in leaving Ralph Andrews Productions. We talked about the gang working together on new projects, and Larry and I tried developing shows together in the hopes of forming our own production company. Instead, Larry partnered with Gary Bernstein. While they did sell some shows, they also kept the lawyers busy, specifically with a lawsuit involving Columbia Television and Paramount Television over their series *Anything for Money*. And then there was an ill-fated attempt at a game show series based on the board game *Yahtzee*, *taped* in Atlantic City, that found Larry and Gary detained by authorities for three hours over rumors they had stolen items from the set. It's my understanding the celebrities who appeared on *Yahtzee*, hosted by Peter Marshall, were never paid because the production company ran out of money.

In 1989, after several years of not working with Larry, he called and asked if I could help him find some improv actors to work with him on a pilot for a Fox Television show titled *Totally Hidden Video*.

I asked my then-boyfriend Randall to join me at a church in Van Nuys where the hidden camera segment was to take place. Here was the simple premise: I told Randall we were going to my friend's wedding. Keep in mind; we were all actors, not civilians. We were aware of the cameras and that this scenario was staged. When it came to the part of the ceremony where the pastor says, "Does anybody object to these two people being wed," all hell broke loose, and Randall was accused of sleeping with the bride. Eventually, the truth was revealed: he was on *Totally Hidden Video*, and we all had a good laugh. We were told this segment would never air, and that it was just a demo to help sell the show. We did it for free to help out Larry. What happened next was a nightmare.

On June 4, 1989, I was driving home when my car was t-boned. It was a severe car accident, you know, the kind when your car spins around, then catches on fire, and it is crushed, and you have to crawl out the window of the driver's side. My pelvis was broken, and I was lucky to be alive. I was ordered to have complete bed rest. A few weeks later, I got a call from Larry. He said to expect a call from a lawyer at Fox. Alan Funt, the creator of the iconic show *Candid Camera*, was suing Larry and his business partner Gary Bernstein, and they needed statements from Randall and me. I told him Randall was in Hawaii on a business trip, and I could barely move. He pleaded with me to meet him immediately at an office building on Lankershim Blvd in North Hollywood, where the Fox attorneys and several executives would be waiting for me. He wouldn't tell me what was going on, but he said, "Just tell the truth."

I put on a loose-fitting dress, tied my hair into a bun, and, using a cane, limped to my car. When I arrived at the unlit parking lot, I was met by a security guard who scared the hell out of me. I remember asking if I could park my car closer to the back door and was told no. I slowly walked into the building and asked to talk to Larry. Again, I was told no. Shit was getting real! I was then ushered into an office that resembled a police station interrogation room, where I was met by three men and the President of Fox Television, Peter Chernin. Had I known Chernin would be there, I would have put some makeup on my bruised face. As it was, I could see what little career I had was being flushed down the toilet. They asked questions for about an hour, asking how I got involved with the hidden camera segment, rephrasing the same questions over and over. I answered truthfully, but the lawyers were beginning to wear me down. The questions became more specific, asking me exactly what time I arrived, how long I was there, and what did Mr. Hovis tell me to do? I finally said, "Listen, guys, I've been on drugs for a few weeks. I'm in pain. I came here as a courtesy, and I'm very tired, so may I leave now?" I told them I could continue answering questions another day, but I never heard from them again. From what I could surmise, there could be more to the story. The segment was shown to the Fox executives and their lawyers. It had been presented to them by Larry as an authentic, hidden camera prank-but this tape proved otherwise. Larry and Gary were fired, ending Larry's career as a game show writer/producer.

A few years later, Gary approached my agent, Fred Wostbrock, to see if I was available to host a cable show that was taped in Las Vegas titled *Surprise Gardner*. I was reticent, but Gary apologized for what had happened years earlier, and for some reason, I trusted him. Well, I guess you know where this story is going. Gary, to save money, bought a block of airline tickets under the name of their first host, actress Shelley Taylor Morgan. She wasn't doing the show any longer. So Gary, to avoid paying extra to have the tickets transferred into my name, said I should tell Southwest Airlines I had married and changed my surname. This way, Gary could use the existing tickets. I guess the real reason I got the job wasn't for my brilliant hosting abilities. It was because I had the same first name as the last gal!

We began taping at a lovely home in Las Vegas that had a plain, dirt backyard. I interviewed an older Black couple about their house as part of the introduction. The script had me telling the couple we were sending them away for the day, and when they returned, we would reveal the surprise landscaping job. Since they were senior citizens, the production company allowed them to wait in the living room all day to be comfortable. A few hours into the job, I spoke to the couple and asked if they were excited to see how great their yard would look in a few short hours. The man said, "This isn't our house. We're actors they hired for the day to pretend this was our home." Fuck! Here I was again, in another phony camera setup! I got Agent Fred on the phone and said to get me out of my contract. What a flim-flam scam! Years later, I learned from one of the other executive producers the home belonged to one of Gary's friends, and he had arranged to have their landscaping done for free for the show.

From internship to interrogation, I learned a lot--like what goes into the structure of a game show and how much teamwork plays into a healthy work environment when there is little else but creativity and elbow grease to bring a concept to fruition. But most of all, I learned what not to do: not to be blinded by arrogance or seduced by greed or to be so desperate as to ruin the lives and livelihoods of people you care about. Those are the lessons that stay with me to this day.

Chapter Fifteen

SADIE, SANFORD & SINATRA

Friday nights were the best night to work. The stages were alive with music and laughter from *The Tonight Show* or sitcoms, including *Chico and the Man* and *Sanford and Son.*

Most shows had a VIP list, but one woman was the most welcome VIP of them all, Sadie O'Sullivan. She was a senior citizen who took the bus from Coldwater Canyon Drive and Ventura Boulevard in Studio City. Then she'd change bus lines several times, traveling six miles by herself so she could attend every taping of both *Hollywood Squares* and *Sanford and Son*, where the casts and crews of the shows adored her. She always brought homemade oatmeal cookies to give the Pages and prided herself on making them without sugar, as she had diabetes and wanted all of us to be mindful of our diets. It was a kind gesture, but they tasted like oatmeal-covered hockey pucks. Sadie was Jewish and regretted the day she married Mr. O'Sullivan. All she'd ever say about him was he was a drinker. Sadie divorced him shortly before their son was born but kept the surname. She never remarried and was an extremely independent woman with a charming smile. I once asked Sadie to show me a photo of her son, and, beaming with pride, she took out her wallet and showed me his picture. He looked like he was in his sixties and as old as her! On the evenings I worked *Squares* and *Sanford*, I would drive Sadie back to her home so she wouldn't have to take the bus.

Redd Foxx always considered Sadie to be his good luck charm. But she wasn't the first mature woman to be regarded as a good luck omen for a show's success. In the early days of television, there was Lillian Miller, affectionately known to TV audiences as Miss Miller. She often sat in the audience at TV tapings dating back to *The Steve Allen Plymouth Show,* as well current programs, like *The Merv Griffin Show* and *The Carol*

Burnett Show. TV show tickets were always free, so going to a taping was a great way to be entertained for a couple of hours. Now that I think back on it, Miss Miller always looked like a little old lady in her heavy winter coat and sensible shoes. She died in 1990, just a month short of her 93rd birthday. Miss Miller became a minor celebrity in her own right, known for being a regular audience member, but not for long. Miss Miller was informed that, because she was often seen and talked to on camera by Merv, she'd have to join the actor's union AFTRA. When production companies discovered they'd have to pay her, she got much less airtime.

Sadie never wanted to appear on camera. She just wanted something to do and to see her NBC friends. Tommy Patino, who worked as the CB on *Sanford and Son*, remembered Sadie well. From time to time, Redd, who had a soft spot in his heart for his number one fan, would slip Sadie a $100 bill. Often, Redd would also give Tommy $100, with instructions to take the Pages who also worked the show across the street and buy them food and drinks.

One evening, while waiting for the taping of *Sanford* to begin, Sadie waved me over to ask what all the commotion was on the stage next door. I explained that the extra electricity in the air was caused by one of Johnny's guests, Frank Sinatra. Without a moment's hesitation, she said, "Sinatra bailed me out of jail once." Astonished, I looked at this petite lady as she proceeded to tell me how she became a wanted woman.

Years earlier, Sadie was at home watching television. She was shocked when a newscaster reported on a gathering of Nazis at The Sportsman's Lodge in Studio City, CA, directly across the street from her apartment. This news was more than Sadie could tolerate. She grabbed her purse, barged into their meeting, and proceeded to hit a Nazi with her handbag. After Sadie got off a few choice words, she was handcuffed and taken to jail. She was fingerprinted and put into a holding cell. Less than an hour after she was put in the slammer, a police officer called out her name. He said that her bail had been posted, and she was free to go. She told the policeman there must be a mistake because no one knew she was in jail, not even her son. The policeman walked Sadie over to the front desk, where he handed her a telegram that read, "Way to go, Sadie. Signed, Francis Albert." The telegram was from Francis Albert Sinatra.

Sadie went on to say she never got to thank Mr. Sinatra for getting her out of jail. I've always cherished senior citizens and knew I had to do something. There was no way in the world I could get close to Mr. Sinatra or his entourage, but I did have what Hayley Mills said in the 1966 film *The Trouble With Angels*, a "Scathingly brilliant idea!"

While Pages work in close proximity to stars, we remained professional at all times. Well, most of the time. I left Sadie's side and knocked on Redd Foxx's dressing room door minutes before he was ready to tape that evening's show. Redd was one of the stars that executives handled like a prized Fabergé egg. At times, he could be uncooperative. Legend has it Redd was upset that Johnny Carson asked for and got a large picture window in his office. Redd wanted one, too. So when the NBC brass dragged their collective feet, he suddenly had to take some sick days. A lot of sick days. The kind of sick days that make executives sit up and take notice. Redd got his window. Before his monumental success as junk dealer Fred Sanford, Redd was best known as a raunchy comic who made the kind of party albums parents would hide from their children. He didn't like to rehearse and performed many of his scenes sitting in a ratty-looking chair. Redd also relied heavily on cue cards while taping. As soon as the show was finished taping, Redd would take a waiting helicopter from NBC to the Burbank airport, all of about four miles, hop a plane to Las Vegas, then perform a midnight show at Thunderbird Hotel. The last thing he needed was a perky little Page bothering him before going out to greet four hundred people waiting in the audience to see him.

But there I was, gently knocking on Redd's dressing room door. Redd opened the door, obviously not expecting to see me. I introduced myself as Sadie's friend, hoping he wouldn't be upset with me. I then asked if he knew Frank Sinatra because not everybody in show business knows everybody (or likes everybody). I proceeded to tell him the Sadie Nazi story, and without hesitation, Redd held up the taping of his show to escort Sadie backstage to Frank Sinatra's dressing room so she could meet him. They chatted a bit, and Frank got a kick out of meeting her.

On the drive back to her apartment, I asked Sadie if she got Frank's autograph, and she said no. Redd was already late taping his show, and she didn't want to take up too much of their time.

Chapter Sixteen

WHAT YOU DIDN'T SEE AT THE EMMYS

My first limo run was a doubleheader. I was assigned to meet comedienne Imogene Coca at her hotel, then whisk her to the Trousdale home of The King of Sketch Comedy, Sid Caesar. That evening, they would be presenters at our final destination, the 1977 Prime Time Emmy Awards Show at the Pasadena Civic Auditorium. It's a magnificent old theatre, with lots of dressing rooms and quick-change areas for the talent. Being the total TV nerd I am, this was the best limo run I could have hoped for! Their groundbreaking variety series, *Your Show of Shows*, was a precursor to *Saturday Night Live*. Imogene starred in the short-lived series *Grindl*, about a single gal who works at many wacky temp jobs. I could identify with that.

Imogene could not have been more...Imogene. She was a delightful pixie of a mature woman who still found every moment of life fresh and exciting. She bragged to me that the gown she was wearing was one she'd first worn to the Emmys in the fifties. When we picked up Sid, he was wearing an older, slightly tattered tuxedo. He climbed into the back seat with Imogene, and as I looked over my shoulder from the front seat of the limo, I couldn't help thinking how they looked like the vintage topper of a wedding cake. Imogene immediately started chatting and giggling and laughing. Sid was gruff and didn't seem to like being trapped in a limo with the chatterbox. He asked Imogene to stop talking, but I don't think she was capable, and after all the years she spent with Sid, I don't think she cared what he said.

Unlike most arrivals, we didn't walk the red carpet because Imogene and Sid were surprise presenters. We were ushered into the side entrance and were hidden in a little tented holding area just off stage left. My job was to make sure they were comfortable, get them a beverage, show them to the restrooms, and whatever they needed. I was their personal Page.

At most award shows, actors seated in the audience were escorted by a Page backstage two commercial breaks before they were due on camera to present an award. This gave the actors time to familiarize themselves with the copy they'd be reciting from the teleprompter, learn to pronounce names, touch up their makeup, and be ready to make their entrance. One of the stars, Suzanne Pleshette, best known for her role as Emily on *The Bob Newhart Show,* was already seated in the holding area. Imogene saw her and told me Suzanne had once referred her to a dentist, but she couldn't remember the dentist's name. She asked if I could go over and ask Suzanne his name. An odd request, but okay. So, I introduced myself and said, "Imogene Coca asked me..." and before I was finished, Ms. Pleschette replied, in that marvelous, deep voice of hers, "She wants to know where I got my caps done! She's asked a dozen times and can't remember." With that, she crossed the room to give Imogene a big hug, and the two threw their heads back, laughing and gossiping.

Some more prominent stars didn't want to sit in the cavernous auditorium for hours, waiting for their names to be announced. Those stars would also hang around the backstage greenroom, helping themselves to generous amounts of food and adult beverages. Pete was entrusted to make sure Neil Diamond got to his assigned seat during the commercial break before his category was announced. In what he admits was a big screw-up, Pete plopped Neil Diamond down in the wrong seat, and when his name was announced as a nominee, the camera operators couldn't find him. Pete was mortified, but Neil remained unfazed, even asking Pete if he could get him a joint. Pete was able to procure the joint, and a month later, much to his surprise, he received a Neil Diamond tour jacket as a thank-you gift.

The show began, and I was backstage, living my dream, live at The Emmys, taking it all in. It all moved so quickly. Once an actor received their Emmy, a Page would escort them through a series of hallways to the ice skating rink (covered with wood and carpeting for the evening) adjacent to the theater. The press would be waiting to photograph the winners with their winged trophies and conduct brief interviews. It was a simpler time when the press mainly asked, "How are you feeling?" not "Who are you wearing?"

There were TV monitors backstage, so while I couldn't see the show live from the audience's point of view, I could catch bits and pieces as I tended to my icons. Early in the show, I heard a thunderous reaction from the audience. Diana Hyland's name was announced as the winner of Outstanding Supporting Actress in a Drama or Comedy Special for her role in the TV movie *The Boy in the Plastic Bubble*. She was given this award posthumously, as she had died from breast cancer at age forty-one a few short months earlier. Her son in the movie, John Travolta, became her real-life sweetheart, and he accepted the award on her behalf. John, clutching the Emmy with a large photo of Diana over his shoulder, said through his tears, "Wherever you are, Diana, I love you," he said, "You did it, baby!"

John exited stage right and sank into a folding chair. He continued crying uncontrollably. I ran over to the makeup area and grabbed a fistful of Kleenex, and raced back to John's side. I tapped him on the shoulder and offered the tissues to him. He nodded to me, took the tissues, then hugged me around my waist, trembling and sobbing, holding me tighter and tighter. I looked down at him and said, "You wanna get out of here?" As he looked up at me, his eyes filled with puddles of tears, and he nodded yes. I found an unoccupied dressing room and hid John there, guarding the door until he felt ready to go to the press area. Of course, people were looking for him, but I kept them away. Once he'd composed himself, we held hands, and I escorted him to the ice rink. I asked if he was sure he was ready, and he said yes, thanked me, and gave my hand a little squeeze.

I went back to the little tent to check on Imogene and Sid as they got their touch-ups to go on camera. Imogene was a bit concerned her older dress might be a little tight, but she took a deep breath as she and Sid made their entrance to thunderous applause. They were a hit! When their segment concluded, they walked backstage only to have Imogene's entire zipper tear away from her fabulous fifties frock and her dress busted open! Sid offered his tuxedo jacket to her. It was a sweet gesture.

I breathed a sigh of relief as Imogene and Sid left the ceremony. My job with them was complete. At that exact moment, another limo pulled up with another surprise guest, Alfred Hitchcock. He was very old and moved extremely slowly. I had done my senior paper at Cal State Northridge on Hitchcock. Could I really be meeting him? I helped my fellow Page, Jeff Garrett, walk with Hitchcock as we tried to get him to the center of the stage before the curtains opened on live television. It was dark backstage, and there were cables and pieces of scenery we needed to navigate through rather quickly. I didn't want to appear to be anything less than professional, so I didn't engage Hitchcock in conversation. But, he did turn to me as I was holding his left arm (and what seemed like half his body weight) and said, "You're doing a very good job." I took my cue from him and said, "I did my senior paper on you. Ask me anything about you." He smiled that mischievous smile as Jeff and I got him to his mark seconds before the world saw the Master of Macabre make his entrance.

Chapter Seventeen

DELLA & CHUCK BARRIS

I need to preface this by telling of my pre-Page adventures with Chuck Barris Productions. While still in high school, I was a contestant on *The Dating Game* twice. I selected the dates and was awarded a dream vacation to San Diego on the first show, and to Paradise Island in The Bahamas the second time. I remember kissing my bachelor on the cheek on the second show and asking, "Where are the Bahamas?" I never met Chuck or had a second date with either of my bachelors, but I did date one of the guys on the staff, Vince Longo. We went out for what was one of the best nights of my life when we saw the live stage production of *The Rocky Horror Show,* starring Tim Curry, at The Roxy on the Sunset Strip.

Chuck already had a reputation as the bad boy of daytime television. He shook up tired, stodgy formats and made relationship shows must-see TV. Chuck has been credited as the innovator of what is now called Reality Television with a list of twelve game shows, including *The Newlywed Game, How's Your Mother-In-Law, The Family Game,* and *3's a Crowd.* Chuck was the only game show producer to have a TV series on all the networks and in syndication simultaneously. Chuck had twenty-seven half-hours of on-air programming at this peak in one week.

When I began my job at NBC, *The Gong Show* was already in production, but it wasn't the iconic show most people remember. John Barbour, a local TV media critic, soon to be one of the stars of NBC's *Real People,* and *Laugh-In* announcer Gary Owens were the original hosts for the network and syndicated versions of the show. For the uninitiated, *The Gong Show* was a parody of tired old talent shows with a panel of three celebrity judges, the regulars being Jaye P. Morgan, Jamie Farr, and Artie Johnson. The judges would bang a large gong if the acts weren't deemed worthy of the show's grand prize of $516.32 or $712.05 on the syndicated version. Announcer Johnny Jacobs, a voice familiar to fans of other Barris Productions, including *The Newlywed Game*, would introduce each show by saying, "From Hollywood, almost live, it's The Gong Show." The band, fronted by Milton Delugg, was named "The Band with a Thug." A beautiful, tall blonde, Sivi Aberg, would be there to hand the act with the most votes an oversized check. Then, confetti would fall, and everyone danced as the credits played. Sometimes Jerry Marden (known as the Munchkin who handed the lollipop to Dorothy in the film *The Wizard of Oz*), would run across the stage, chased by a man carrying a butterfly net and dressed as a doctor. His name was Tony Cacciotti and years later, he married actress Valerie Harper.

As zany as the show was trying to be, it wasn't catching on with viewers. Something was missing. Turns out, the missing link was Chuck Barris.

To avoid cancellation and fulfill his vision of *The Gong Show:* a fun-filled half-hour featuring entertaining acts combined with...whatever, Chuck took the reins as host of both the daytime and nighttime versions. Chuck was now able to produce the show on camera, ratcheting up the energy, and injecting a sillier sense of humor. As a result, a phenomenon was born. People either loved it or hated it, but everyone was talking about it! Demand for tickets exceeded our limited capabilities. Rather than changing the audience after the second or third taping during the meal break, Pages were told to bring a new audience in after each show to avoid a riot. The show tapings on Thanksgiving weekend were the roughest, and I'm told the Pages went across the street for margaritas between shows because they were so wiped out!

Now, big stars like David Letterman and Steve Martin wanted to be judges. Steve also appeared in a comedic moment with a prop arrow in his head, playing the banjo. Chuck amped up the irreverence as the host, forsaking wearing a traditional tuxedo, instead making his entrances in blue jeans with a silly hat pulled down around his eyes, as he told people going into a commercial break, "We'll be back with more stuff right after this message." Fun Fact: Chuck and Milton Delugg co-wrote *The Gong Show* theme song.

Vince and I were no longer dating, just friends, and he would invite me to watch the acts audition in a building near Hollywood Boulevard and Cahuenga. It was excruciating! I don't know who it was harder to see get rejected by the producers: the people who thought they truly were talented or the wackos who were too avant-garde even for *The Gong Show!* Chuck was usually at the auditions, strumming his guitar, looking for the diamond in the rough he could turn into TV gold. I also became a regular around the office, helping Chuck and the writers with game show run-thrus. I would play a contestant, and they would not only test the concept of a show but, if needed, they'd have us answer trivia questions. Most of the shows were personality-driven, so I didn't have to be smart, I just had to talk and have fun. In the summer, we'd also gather at Warner Brother Studios in Burbank, where Geoff Edwards hosted the syndicated version of another of Chuck's non-traditional game shows, *The New Treasure Hunt.*

I met Geoff years ago through my cousin, who worked with him at radio station KMPC in Los Angeles. Geoff suggested I join him working with an improv comedy group on Monday nights. He said it would be a good way to help me become a writer, and not to be intimidated in show biz situations. He was right about the writing, but I've never been the kind of gal who gets intimidated.

Geoff's improv training, and years as a top Los Angeles radio personality, were a natural fit for a show filmed on the fly. Here's how the game was played: a contestant would select one of the thirty colorful boxes of all shapes and sizes. Then, the taping would stop, and Geoff would head backstage to huddle with the writers and producers, going over key points of the upcoming comedy bit. Geoff would have to do a lot of fast-talking, tormenting the contestant who picked a box to see if they wanted cash or what was in the box. Geoff couldn't use cue cards while playing the game because the contestants would be able to read along to see what would come next and, well, spoil the surprise, which would make for bad television. The show was like *Let's Make a Deal* on acid.

Lunch was always great at the *Treasure Hunt* tapings. Chuck would order a few twelve-foot-long sandwiches with lots of salads and sweets.

He'd play the guitar and just hang with everybody in an area that looked like the Town Square of Anytown USA, complete with a gazebo. A few people would grab a golf cart and sneak off to the outdoor set of *The Waltons* to get high. In all the years I was in Chuck's company, I never saw him do drugs or drink. When he wasn't in his producer or host mode, Chuck was a sweet, mellow guy. He was just a guy from Philly, my hometown, who liked to make people smile. Chuck was a hugger. Just a hugger, not a perv.

As *The Gong Show* began to evolve or devolve depending on your sense of humor, Chuck started to populate the show with reoccurring guests. Comic Murray Langston, a guy with a brown paper bag over his head, became an overnight sensation as The Unknown Comic. When Chuck needed to kill some time because he'd run out of acts for the day, he grabbed one of the stagehands, like Gene Patton. The crew at NBC called him "Hat," but Chuck nicknamed him "Gene, Gene, The Dancing Machine." Seeing Gene do his unique dance style, shuffling his feet and tipping his hat to the tune of Count Basie's *"Jumping' At the Woodside,"* was pure joy.

There were more than a few future stars who were featured on the show. Paul Reubens was one half of a duo who sang while on their tiptoes, called Suave & Debonair. He would go on to film and television fame as Pee-wee Herman. There were The Mystic Knights of the Oingo Boingo, who would later drop the Mystic Knights from their name. One of their band members, Danny Elfman, became a multi-Academy Award nominee and Emmy award-winning composer. Another Oscar nominee and Emmy winner, Mare Winningham, sang *"Here, There and Everywhere,"* receiving a standing ovation from a guy who knows a thing or two about music, Paul Williams. *Police Academy* star Michael Winslow received thirty points, the most that could be awarded, for creating dozens of amazing sounding sound effects using only his mouth and a microphone. In 1976, Andrea McArdle won the hearts of the judges before winning the title role of *Annie* on Broadway.

Chuck even included me in one of his spontaneous on-air bits. Here's what happened. I was giving a tour when someone from the Page staff ran up to me and said, "I'm taking over your tour. Chuck Barris wants to see you now!" I thought something was wrong and ran to the stage, only to find a giddy Chuck. He told me not to ask any questions, but when the curtain went up at the start of the show, to just walk out and shake hands with the other women going on stage. I said, "When?" and he said, "Watch, you'll know when." Okay then. I was standing with a few other women who worked at NBC, sound engineers, set painters, all from different departments. With the opening theme music blaring, the curtain went up, and there was Chuck saying something like, "I'd like you to meet the women who work at NBC." That was our cue! We all turned to each other and shook each other's hands as though we were meeting for the first time. That was the whole bit, my fifteen seconds of fame!

I think Chuck took a liking to me, in a brotherly, sisterly way, because I reminded him of his daughter, Della. Heck, she reminded me of me! She was fresh-faced, shy, and an unapologetic daddy's girl. Chuck was divorced and had recently gained full-time custody of Della, who was his only child. *The Gong Show* taped on the weekend, allowing the father and daughter to drive into work together in Chuck's Mercedes 450SL with a license plate that read "Della." She wore jeans and baggy clothes and ran her fingers through her tousled ash-blonde air, covering her face when she was embarrassed by the antics going on around her. This had to be the ultimate Take Your Daughter to Work Day experience. Della was Alice in a weird Wonderland.

As the weeks and months went by, I could see Della was coming out of her shell. The make-up people would add glitter to her eyes and gloss to her lips. Della began wearing silly hats, like her dad, or sparkly berets, like those worn by *Gong Show* regular panelist Jaye P. Morgan. She had the run of the studio but was never one of those spoiled show-biz kids. Occasionally, she would introduce Chuck at the show's opening, saying, "And now the host and star of the show, my daddy!" She was sweet and fun and genuinely curious about all aspects of the show. She followed her dad around like a puppy dog, which he loved. He would proudly introduce her to the celebrities on the panel, the crew, and the studio audience, and she would be beaming.

Many attractive women were around the set, some of whom were strippers from the local gentleman's clubs. They were brought in to do silly acts that were intended to be gonged, but at least they'd look sexy. I began to see a difference in Della when Chuck started to date Robin Altman, nicknamed Red. She wasn't like the other performers. She was more like a fashion model, tall, thin, and it didn't seem like she cared about wearing a bra. Red was beautiful and understated in her white silk blouse and tight pants. She had a megawatt smile and the perfect amount of feathering in her Farrah Fawcett-like hairdo. Chuck was smitten with Red, and they became inseparable in the studio. I think it was only natural for Della to be a bit jealous of the time Chuck was spending with Red, and in a bid to appear more grown-up, Della's eye make-up got heavier, and she became more independent. I never saw her drink or use drugs, but others did, and there was cause for concern.

In 1980, Chuck starred in, directed, and co-wrote with Robert Downey, Sr. *The Gong Show Movie*. The thin plotline involved Chuck having a nervous breakdown over the stress of people constantly auditioning for him at inopportune times. Spoiler alert: His *Gong Show* family gathers as they sing him back to sanity with a rousing little ditty, written by Chuck Barris, titled, *"Don't Get Up For Me"*. The film received an R rating and featured uncensored footage from the TV series, including Jaye P. Morgan exposing her breasts. The film was a box office bomb and was pulled from theaters after three days.

In his own words, Chuck said he was having a "mid-life crisis on national television." Della, who had been unhappy living with her father full time, asked Chuck if she could move out of his home to live on her own. Chuck took Della, at the age of sixteen, to see a psychiatrist. The decision was made to let Della move out and have access to her trust fund. Chuck has said on numerous occasions he regrets that decision. "I think I really screwed up." Tired of the critics, tired of the adoration, and just plain tired, Chuck ended the show and moved to France with Red, and without Della.

I lost touch with Della. So did her dad. So did a lot of people who cared about her. This was the era of Tough Love when professionals advised parents, loved ones, and friends to cut off communication and finances with the addict in the hopes they'd either hit rock bottom or reach out to get the help they needed to remain sober. In 1988, Chuck, now living in New York, and Della reconciled. Chuck made plans to fly to Los Angeles to see Della, but she was found dead in her home the day before Chuck's flight. She was only thirty-six.

In Chuck's words, from his book *Della: A Memoir of My Daughter*, "I'm told by friends that Della was very depressed just before she died. Of course, she was depressed. She was sick. She was broke. And she was burdened with a low-life lover who provided her with drugs, and aided and abetted her depression. Della drank too much vodka, snorted too much cocaine, and died just like the death certificate said she did: from an excessive amount of everything. I don't think Della wanted to die. I think she made a horrible mistake." Della had also tested HIV positive.

In the decades since *The Gong Show* has been off the air, others have tried to capture the show's spirit, balancing the absurd acts with those who were genuinely talented. Chuck never wanted to revive the show. He was done. In 1986, Chuck sold his shares of Chuck Barris Productions to Burt (*Midnight Special*) Sugarman for $86 million. Sony now owns the titles. Both Comic Dave Attell and radio personality Don Bleu's versions failed to capture the public's interest, and an *Extreme Gong Show* hosted by George Gray only lasted one season. ABC tried a bold experiment by joking the joke when selecting a faux host for their summer *Gong Show* series, British comic Tommy Maitland, portrayed by a putty-faced Mike Myers, of *SNL* fame.

Chuck was a broadcasting futurist, always ahead of the curve, pushing the boundaries and paving the way for a new generation of producers and network executives to create television content that could appeal to a younger audience. On March 21, 2017, Chuck died of natural causes in Palisades, New York. In addition to being a game show producer, host, and author, Chuck wrote the Freddie "Boom Boom" Cannon hit song, "*Palisades Park*." It was his first creative success. The catchy pop song peaked at #3 on the Billboard Hot 100 chart the week of June 23–30, 1962, six months before Della was born.

Was Chuck a paid assassin for the CIA, as he claimed in his book *Confessions of a Dangerous Mind*? Did he use his opportunity to chaperon *Dating Game* contestants as the perfect cover for his clandestine assignments? Did he really kill thirty-three people? Leaving people uncertain about what they were seeing or hearing was part of Chuck's genius. Much like Andy Kaufman, decades later, we're still questioning their antics-secretly hoping Andy is still alive and Chuck is living happily ever after, strumming his guitar, in the witness relocation program.

Chapter Eighteen

FREDDIE PRINZE

June 22, 1954 – January 29, 1977

On December 6, 1973, in 325 seconds on *The Tonight Show*, a superstar was born, Freddie Prinze. Johnny waved him over, and a new Prinze of Comedy was crowned. Freddie became the first stand-up to sit down next to Johnny following his debut performance on the late-night show. The applause continued for another thirty seconds, and the audience fell in love with the tall, dark, and handsome nineteen-year-old. He almost didn't make it on the show that night. Talent coordinator Craig Tennis said Fred de Cordova told him, "He's not going on. I hate the way he looks. Johnny's going to hate him. I'm canceling him right now." Lucky for us, de Cordova didn't get his way. Johnny gave Freddie a nice introduction, not too flowery, very welcoming: "This is his first appearance on the Tonight Show, so make him feel welcome. You sound like you're in a good mood. Would you welcome Freddie Prinze? Freddie?"

Freddie opened with a joke to let people know a bit about himself. "I come from two backgrounds. Hungarian and Puerto Rican. I'm a Hungarican. I could never figure out how my parents met, a gypsy and a Puerto Rican. I asked my mother, she said on the subway, they were trying to pick each other's pockets. My mother used to talk about the wedding. 'Oh, it was beautiful. You should have been there.' I was." And, if that wasn't enough, he told a joke with a punchline that would become his million-dollar catchphrase, "Ees not my job, man." Johnny invited him back for another appearance on the show and Freddie, proving he can think fast and funny on the spot, said, "I'd love to. Same audience?"

While Freddie was new to television audiences, he was known by the top comics of the day, who helped mentor him in the comedy clubs.

The comics included such well-known stand-ups as David Brenner, Jimmie "JJ" Walker, and future Tonight Show host Jay Leno. Freddie and Jay were roommates, and Jay taught Freddie, a native New Yorker, how to drive.

Television Producer James Komak (*The Courtship of Eddie's Father, Welcome Back, Kotter*) called Craig Tennis the following day and said he'd found the lead for a script he was developing titled *Chico and the Man.* The man cast to be The Man was Academy Award-winning actor Jack Albertson. Albertson was known to a younger generation as Grandpa Joe in the Gene Wilder film *Willy Wonka and The Chocolate Factory.* As beloved as Albertson was in that film (and in-person), this time, he played mechanic Ed Brown, a total curmudgeon. But then he meets Chico Rodriguez, a street-smart Chicano young man who uses humor to soften Ed's rough edges. It was an immediate hit! And so were Freddie's tight jeans.

When I got to NBC, Freddie was one of the network's biggest stars and also one of the biggest rascals in the building. He would wreak havoc in the halls, randomly answering the phones using different voices, and pretending to be various characters. Sometimes he'd just pick up the receiver, then immediately hang up. Freddie always took a moment to say hello to the tour groups and entertained the audience between scenes at the taping of his show. He could also be seen engaging in spontaneous touch football games in the wide hallways.

I once got caught in the crossfire of a food fight with Freddie. He didn't aim well, and when Freddie flung a pie, it landed on my face and uniform. He was apologetic and immediately ran into the restroom to grab paper towels, handing some to me, then using the rest to clean the floor and walls. I assured him I was okay and that my uniform was indestructible, and we had a good laugh.

Tommy Patino remembers the time he was standing at the urinal when Freddie Prinze came into the bathroom, stood next to him, and said, "I guess this is where all the dicks hang out." Tom worked *Chico and the Man* often and noticed a decisive change in Freddie as the week of rehearsing and taping progressed: "On Monday, he'd come in looking pretty bad, twice his age, but I'll tell you what, by Friday, he looked clean-cut raring to go."

When I asked former NBC Page Beth Rees if she had any Freddie stories, she was reluctant to talk about them. Then memories she'd long ago suppressed came back to her. She said she wanted Freddie presented in a good light and that her "silly story" should be included. She was a good acquaintance and didn't want to presume to be more than that. Freddie had his pick of women at the time, including a serious relationship with Kitty Bruce, the daughter of legendary comic Lenny Bruce.

Beth said her experiences with Freddie were "85 percent positive. He had a lead foot and a zest for life that bordered on suicidal even in a car. He taught me to play backgammon using the dreaded doubling cube, and we gambled with M&M's instead of cash." Jack Albertson let Beth and Freddie use his dressing room for their backgammon games. Jack wanted Freddie to have a place to relax where no one could find him, and the phone wouldn't constantly ring off the hook. Beth wasn't into drugs and lent a sense of normality to Freddie's hedonistic lifestyle. "As truly, truly fond as I was of him, even at the time, I knew something wasn't quite right. But I couldn't quantify it. I spent so much quality time with him that I never really even thought about it. So stupid! The restaurant he took my mom and me to in Glendale, where I had my apartment, was called Shenanigans. I loved that! As fond as I was of him, I have to say that he was perhaps not an unwilling victim. Heck, he was twenty-two. So was I. He made fun of the fact I was three months older than he was. He called me his 'elder sister.' And 'Cousin Beth.' I have not thought about this for so long."

Pete Hammond saw Freddie on what would be Freddie's the last day at the studio. He was assigned to give a VIP tour of the facility. One of the stops along the way was observing what would be the final rehearsal of *Chico and The Man* with Freddie.

Pete had met Freddie escorting him through the gauntlet of electronic press reporters at the Sheraton Universal. "I picked up Freddie at his home in a limo in the early morning. He said goodbye to his wife and infant child and was moody. Once we got there, he was so excited, raring to go, and we zipped him through twenty-six affiliate promotional interviews and were done by 12:30. He said to say hi to him if I ever saw him around NBC. I did, but he didn't remember me. He seemed sad and bored during the rehearsal that day."

It turns out there was a much darker side to Freddie. Still working as a Page, aspiring to be a comedy writer, Linda Levinson befriended Freddie and began submitting jokes to him. One of the jokes she sold to Freddie was, "I went to the Schick Center to stop smoking. Now, I can't stop shaving."

Linda recalled, "At least he paid better than Joan Rivers, at fifteen dollars a joke."

Linda was with Freddie the night of his last show at The Improv on Melrose, where the audience loved him. "On stage, he had been lucid. I didn't know if he was stoned, but he didn't act like it," said Linda. Freddie didn't want the night to end, so he invited Linda and her friend Janet back to an apartment with his friend, Alan Bursky. Alan got into Freddie's blue Corvette as Janet and Linda followed in Janet's green Camaro. At the apartment, they made small talk, and Linda remembers being astonished when Freddie told her he had done nine Quaaludes in one day. He showed Linda a brown bottle with an eye-dropper and boasted he also did liquid cocaine, which, unbeknownst to him, was a placebo. Someone in his inner circle was trying to get him clean.

As the night went on, Freddie got more and more depressed. He told Linda, "When I'm in Vegas, do you know that I make seventy-five thousand dollars? My agent gets ten percent, my manager gets twenty percent, the publicist gets some amount, and I walk away with five grand." Linda went on to say, "Wait a minute! That's still a lot of money. Your car is paid for, what do you need? Isn't everything taken care of?" Freddie said, "That's all I get. Everyone wants a piece of me." Linda advised him to tell his producer James Komack how he was feeling. "He can get you help." Linda wasn't Freddie's girlfriend or a therapist. She was a comedy writer and was concerned. She said to Freddie, "I make you funnier, and you make me sadder."

He then told her he was going to kill himself the next night and "would I mind going into the bedroom to talk about it?" Linda went with him, and she said, "The minute the door was closed, Freddie said, 'Will you fuck me?' I said, No. Freddie said, 'Oh, I get it. You're not a star-fucker.' To which I said, 'You're not a star. You're a comic!' Freddie then asked, 'Can I beat off in front of you' and he started to unbuckle his pants." Linda didn't want to be denigrated by this painfully uncomfortable moment. "That kind of thing never turned me on. I turned my back to him. I was pissed, and I was thinking, great, it was another guy exposing himself to me, and I really didn't need to see! What is it with guys? Do they think it's so pretty?" Linda, trying to remain calm and not upset Freddie, told him, "I'm going to turn my back to you and smoke a cigarette, and you can do whatever you want in the time it takes for me to smoke this cigarette. But after that, I don't want to ever speak to you again."

Late the next morning, the phone rang. It was Janet, and she was screaming into the phone: "Freddie actually went through with it." Still half asleep, Linda said, "What are you talking about?" "He shot himself! He shot himself!" Janet told her that people were gathering at the UCLA Medical Center for a vigil and asked if Linda wanted to go. "No, I didn't want anything to do with it."

I was home recovering from hepatitis when I got the call: Freddie had shot himself with a .38 caliber pistol, pointed at his right temple. Or so that's how it was first reported. Turns out the initial report wasn't correct. Alan Bursky later reported the weapon was an Astra Constable, a copy of the gun used by James Bond that resembles a Walther PPK. Following extensive surgery, Freddie was placed in the Intensive Care Unit on life support, but the news reports weren't optimistic. Thirty-three hours after he pulled the trigger, surrounded by friends and family, Freddie was taken off life support.

How could Freddie, a new father, one of NBC's brightest stars, a role model to Puerto Rican kids and up-and-coming comics, put a gun to his head? Were there signs he was in trouble? He was separated from his wife and his ten-month-old son, Freddie Prinze, Jr. Two months before his death, Freddie had been arrested for a DUI (Driving Under the Influence), giving fans their first glimpse into Freddie's struggles. Freddie's psychiatrist had prescribed the highly-addictive sedative drug Methaqualone, also known as the recreational drug Quaalude. When used correctly, it helped patients with insomnia and worked as a muscle relaxant. There were also rumors Freddie was abusing alcohol and cocaine. Another factor may have been that Freddie's wife served him with a restraining order on January 26, 1977, the day before he shot himself.

Freddie called several people on what would be his final night: his personal secretary, his psychiatrist, his business manager, Martin "Dusty" Snyder, a few friends, and his estranged wife. Freddie was staying at the Beverly Comstock Hotel, Room 216, on the border of Westwood and Beverly Hills. Friends and family couldn't fathom how the man who seemed to have everything could kill himself. Police initially concluded Freddie's death to be a suicide because a note was found in his room reading, "I must end it. There's no hope left. I'll be at peace. No one had anything to do with this. My decision totally – Freddie Prinze P.S. I'm sorry. Forgive me. Dusty's here. He's innocent. He cared."

In 1982, Prinze's widow, Kathy Cochran, Freddie Prinze, Jr., and his mother, Mary Preutzel (Freddie's last name at birth), settled malpractice suits close to $1 million against the doctors who overprescribed Quaaludes to him.

In addition, it was determined that Freddie was under the influence of drugs at the time of his death, allowing the family to receive money from Freddie's life insurance policies. His death was eventually ruled accidental. His family believed and argued that Freddie, if not for the drugs, "would have been of sound mind and body, that he would not have chosen to leave his young son behind along with his loving parents."

Freddie's casket was placed in a crypt in the Forest Lawn Memorial Park Court of Remembrance overlooking NBC Burbank, where his sitcom was taped and where he guest-hosted the late-night series that launched his career. Celebrities including Lucille Ball, Paul Williams, and Gabe Kaplan were among the mourners. Freddie was eulogized by his distraught co-star, Jack Albertson, and close friend, singer Tony Orlando. Twenty-seven years following his death, Freddie was posthumously awarded a Star on the Hollywood Walk of Fame. The location is 6755 Hollywood Boulevard. His only son, Freddie Jr., who never knew his father, now a movie star in his own right, attended the unveiling star ceremony.

Freddie told many people he wanted to kill himself on numerous occasions. Reports are he tried to kill himself at age seventeen after a breakup with a girl. He often called his friends, like Jimmie "JJ" Walker, to come over to his place in the middle of the night. "So you'd get in the car, and you roll over there. He lived at 7777 Hollywood Boulevard. There would be like ten people there, and you'd say, 'What the hell is this all about?' He said, 'Just wanted to see if you'd come, man.' He would always pull stunts like that. He had a tremendous ego."

Drug rehab centers had yet to become a mainstream choice for addicts who needed to get well, as people were still stigmatized for confronting their diseases. Freddie became a cautionary tale. When Freddie died, several of his close friends were motivated to clean up their acts, and quit drinking and doing drugs.

Some people don't remember Freddie, and some haven't heard of him or seen any of the three seasons Freddie starred in *Chico and The Man*. The character of Chico was funny, and kind, and one-of-a-kind. Surprisingly, the series continued. Jack Albertson paid special tribute to his good friend and co-star. By Season 4, twelve-year-old Gabriel Melgar was brought on to play Raul and verbal joust with Jack Albertson. But the chemistry just wasn't there.

If you haven't already, give yourself a treat and look at videos of Freddie posted on YouTube to see him in action. Pretty soon, you'll find yourself smiling.

Chapter Nineteen

JAY MICHELIS & JOAN RIVERS

Fair warning: this chapter is filled with profanity, drug use, and sexual content,and is entirely politically incorrect. In other words, meet Jay Michelis. Officially, he was the West Coast Vice President for Corporate and Media Relations, and we Pages were part of his responsibilities. Jay himself had been an NBC Page in 1959 at the Sunset and Vine NBC Studios. Jay was smart and funny and as flamboyant as he was indispensable. When there was a problem getting talent to their destination or just keeping them happy so their shows could go on, Jay was the calm in the storm. One afternoon, I saw a full-sized milk chocolate toilet outside his office. Jay had ordered it to give as a gag gift to one of the NBC stars who had royally screwed up. Hence, the throne.

I'd also like to mention that because of Jay's recommendation, Dinah Brein and Marilee Mahoney got their jobs on the Page staff. That was a good thing, as they have become a lifelong friend to us all. Yet, Jay had an odd way of showing he cared about the Page staff.

I guess I felt honored, in a way, that Jay even knew who I was. He bestowed upon me the nickname "Jewess," although he never once discussed religion. Al Ovadia was "Mr. Hole," Courtney was "The WAP," a nod to his Italian heritage. Courtney was not immune to Jay's quick quips, "On a tour, Jay would pick on me. I'd be giving a tour, and he'd walk by and say, 'Mr. Conte, where did you leave your handcuffs?' Or whisper under his breath just loud enough for the guests to hear, 'He's a drug dealer.' If he didn't like you, he didn't pick on you." Jay gave another female coworker the nickname "Miss Tits," Neil Weiner was summoned by the moniker "Mr. Weenie."

Racist, never. Crude, yes! Al Ovadia heard Jay say to a woman, "I see you're wearing a flesh-colored dress." Jeff Mackler heard Jay call out to a Black friend of his by saying, "There's a Black person over there. Oh, Mr.

Black Person?" When a visiting female NBC executive was introduced to the staff by Jay, he said, "And this is the mindless twat from NBC New York." He often sent vinegar over to a table where NBC Compliance and Practice's Susan Simons would be having lunch with friends. It was his douchey way of saying hello to her. *Tonight Show* trumpeter Doc Severinsen was known as "Brass Lips." Jay's friend, comedienne Joan Rivers (married to Edgar Rosenberg), was "Mrs. Rosenjew," and Dorothy Tiano Melvin, Joan's Assistant/Manager, who was dating a man who rode a motorcycle, earned the moniker "Cycle-Slut." Is it odd to say that it was a badge of honor to be given a nickname by Jay?

Jay worked closely with his assistant, Shan Tabor (who he nicknamed "Mrs. Douchebag"), an attractive woman who kept his numerous secrets. Shan could be a bit short with people and also a lot of fun. Sometimes we'd see her driving her dune buggy to work. And, on more than a few occasions, Shan had explained that Jay didn't hate the other Pages or me. It was just his way of talking. Courtney Conte wasn't the only man I spoke to who smiled when thinking of Shan, "Shan Tabor was so hot. I had such a crush on her. She was mean, and I thought she wasn't very nice."

When Shan took the week off before Christmas, Jeff Garrett would be Jay's assistant, attending to the last-minute cards and gifts that needed to be sent. Even working closely with Jay, being invited to dinner at Musso & Frank, and fielding his phone calls didn't make Jeff immune from Jay's nicknames. He referred to Jeff as "Miss Garrett," and to Jeff's father, a man who had suffered a debilitating stroke years earlier as "The Turnip."

Neil worked more closely with Jay than I did. He approached Jay about expanding the Guest Relations area by selling tourist souvenirs-little trinkets like pens, mugs, towels, lapel pins, and key chains. A plan was already in the works, but Neil became the primary person to set up the Specialty Merchandise display in the tour area. While guests waited for their tour, Neil would hold court, and boy, he could sell, sell, sell! I still have my *Hollywood Squares* necklace with a diamond chip in the center square.

Jay was a great defender of his current and former Pages. Some VPs wouldn't hesitate to cover their collective executive asses when a producer called screaming about some supposed infraction or faux pas made by a Page. Jeff Macker moved from the Page staff and worked on a media campaign for the NBC TV movie *Adam* starring Daniel J Travanti. The film told the true sorry of the abduction and murder of Adam, age six, and how his father lobbied to change how law enforcement agencies investigated such crimes. The film's producer, Linda Otto, asked Jeff if he had seen the movie.

"While I had an advanced copy, I chose not to screen it for very personal reasons. Linda asked if I saw it, and I chose not to lie. She went ballistic. 'How can you ever promote a film like this when you haven't seen it?' I explained my reason; (the movie) aired in October 1983 and was about a child being abducted, never to be seen alive again! My first daughter, Courtney, was born in January 1983. To this day, I haven't screened the film! The subject matter was just too much, being a new father. When I got back to my office, Jay asked me to come to his office. He locked the door from the little button on his desk and asked, 'How are things going, Mr. Macker? You came back from a meeting with Mizzzz (emphasis supplied by Jay) Otto, and no sooner did you get in your car on her lot, she called me and wanted me to fire you.' Jay did not suffer fools, and called Ms. Otto back, saying, 'Jeff is a hard worker who did outstanding work in HIS department, and if Jeff believed that he didn't need to see the fucking movie, that was good enough for him! Listen, bitch. He's on my staff, and I will do whatever I want to.' Then, Jay told her to go fuck herself, and he had a good laugh."

Pete Hammond said Jay protected him when an outraged publicist tried to have him fired. There seemed to be a colossal misunderstanding when the publicist got word someone saw his client, a male NBC star, dressed as a woman on a limo run. The story began to snowball until the publicist, only knowing one Page's name, Pete's, accused him of spreading rumors his client was a cross-dresser. Again, Jay, not liking to be told what to do, got to the bottom of the story. He discovered that the male star was wearing a costume on his way to a Halloween party. Jay eviscerated the publicist. Not only that, Jay thought so highly of Pete that he entrusted him to hand-deliver a gift from the network president to Johnny Carson each year on the anniversary of his show.

Tim Danker was sure he would be in big trouble when he sarcastically lamented to some fellow Pages that Jay's last name was hard to pronounce. "What is it, Mickles? Micklus? what is it?" At that precise moment, Jay walked past Tim and said, "Do you have a problem with my name?" and kept walking. Tim thought he was a goner, but Jay never held that remark against him. Years later, when Tim worked as a Unit Manager for NBC, they had an excellent business relationship. Tim and Emily Aiken, a former Page who worked for Jay editing on-air promotional spots, were extended a coveted invitation to Jay's vacation home (Gray Wolf Lodge in Big Sur, California) for his annual Pig Roast. They both have only fond memories of Jay and acknowledge he could be a rascal. Jay was a longtime friend of Courtney's parents. Courtney told me Jay sent his mother a cordless vibrator sex toy as a Christmas gift. "Mom thought it was funny. Dad, not so much. He thought it was insane but eventually laughed about it."

At this point, I must interject that Jay was a magnificent letter writer, both on a personal and corporate level. His letters have been treasured and photocopied by numerous ex-NBC employees, who drag them out to read aloud on special occasions. No one, and I repeat, no one, could get away with this kind of humor now. One former NBC employee told me, "These were inter-office letters. The people who got them were delighted that they were recipients of a Jay Michelis memo because they felt they had a treasure. They were always hysterical, for those people."

I've been told Jay wrote a memo to Brandon Tartikoff, the then President of NBC when he wanted to turn down a request from Bob Hope to get a free RCA Stereo Television Receiver. Jay reminded Brandon that not only was Hope one of the richest men on earth, but he could barely hear in monaural, let alone stereo. Jay continued to criticize Hope, saying he was a horrible husband and father and hadn't a sense of humanity while working for NBC. The letter continued berating Hope, who Jay said managed to make money from three major wars with his television specials, where he entertained our troops. But, since it was near Christmas, if Brandon wanted him to have the stereo, Brandon could sign Jay's note and mark it approved. The actual letter was scathing. I'm telling you the G-Rated version of what was read to me.

Jay sent another typewritten note with a gift to a birthday/housewarming held by Edgar Rosenberg. The note attached requested a nude photo of the family in return. I left out the part of the story where Jay wanted to know if Joan's manager had done sexually suggestive squats on the gift box.

In another correspondence, using sexual innuendo, Jay referred to the husband of one of his best female friends as "Mr. Taco Breath." He mused in another letter about the thought of seeing a former NBC President's wife without her undies, exposing herself by snapping wild beavers at passers-by. Jay wasn't above making disparaging remarks aimed at himself in his letters. Shan ostensibly sent a note (obviously dictated by Jay) to the head of the NBC Commissary requesting that the obese asshole she worked with be given special consideration, as he was going on a diet.

Jay would sometimes end his letters with something amusing like, "from your friends in Talent Relations, Toasters, Tubes" (a subtle jab at our parent company, General Electric). And instead of signing his name, he'd come up with silly pseudonyms like Jesus Sunbeam or would simply write, "Yours in Christ."

For all his humorous brashness and lascivious levity, there was a dark side to Jay, including his involvement in "Memogate." In 1983, after more than proving herself ratings-wise while guest-hosting over eighty *Tonight Show* episodes, Joan was named the permanent guest host of *The Tonight Show*. In a People magazine interview, Joan said she believed NBC would never have given the permanent host spot to a woman. This theory was reinforced when she and Edgar saw an NBC inter-office memo deliberately leaked with a list of all male names. Joan said, "My name wasn't on it at all."

Some doubted there was ever a memo. But Dorothy saw it. "It was signed 'JM,' written in blue ink, with a handwritten added message from

Jay to Joan and Edgar reading, 'You have no home at NBC.' I can still see the signature."

"It was definitely his writing." Dorothy recalled that the memo said, "These are the people we propose to replace Johnny. It was David Brenner, Garry Shandling, some other male comics. They were all people who were funny but didn't pull in Joan's numbers. Letterman wasn't on it. I don't think Jay Leno was on it. Johnny was nowhere near stepping down. The conversation was ridiculous. There was no reason to have a memo saying this is who will replace Johnny when he steps down. It was 1986. Johnny didn't leave for years." (Johnny announced his retirement on May 23, 1991. His last show was May 22, 1992.) Dorothy continued, "There was no way he was leaving. There was no reason for this memo to have happened. I think it was just Jay Michelis being mean and not realizing this was going to take on a life of its own."

Dorothy heard Joan and Edgar having a conversation with Jay on the phone about the memo. "I don't think he realized he was stirring the pot to the extent it got stirred. And then, once it got out of control, once the tiger was loose, there was nothing that could be done about it." I couldn't help but wonder why Joan and Edgar didn't talk directly to Johnny, her biggest champion. Johnny was her mentor. After all, it was Carson Productions who hired Joan as the permanent guest host, not NBC.

Instead, On May 7, 1986, Joan and Edgar announced they secretly cut a three-year deal for $10 million with Fox Television. Joan got her own late-night talk show, and Edgar got his title as an Executive Producer.

Joan was now persona non grata on *The Tonight Show*. According to Dorothy, she saw Peter Lassally, then Producer of *The Tonight Show*, and his wife Alice at the Century City Mall in California. They had been close friends with Joan and Edgar. When asked, Peter said he had never seen the memo. Dorothy was the first to tell him about it. "It was all done very badly, but when I told Peter Lassally about the memo, he was in shock. He said there's no way a memo like that would ever have gone out without his being informed. Peter found out about [Joan's Fox] deal when the news broke. Joan quickly called Peter and said,

'Leave Johnny and come with us.' Peter was very loyal to Johnny, and he was very angry that Joan had done this behind his back. I don't know how it got out. They didn't expect it to get out. She was trying to do damage control. It was too late. She called Johnny immediately. 'Johnny, it's Joan', and he hung up the phone. Johnny never talked to them again."

Five months later, on October 9, 1986, *The Late Show Starring Joan Rivers* premiered, and the booking wars amped up. Here's how it played out: if you were a guest on Joan's show, you wouldn't be asked onto *The Tonight Show*. Seven months into the run, with declining ratings and behind-the-scenes discord, things came to a head when Joan refused to fire her husband Edgar as an Executive Producer. Fox fired them both. About three months later, on August 14, 1987, Edgar was found dead from a drug overdose in a Philadelphia hotel room. His death was ruled a suicide.

"Jay was mean. There was no real friendship," said Dorothy. "He called the morning of Edgar's funeral and asked me to tell Mrs. Rosenjew that he would not be coming to the funeral because he was at his incredibly expensive house in Glendale and would be out driving his incredible car." She continued, "Jay was like a good friend you have fun with, but never turn your back on. There are so many people like Jay Michelis, so much fun to be with, and you really believe that he's a trustworthy friend when the entire time he was a total snake."

There is another letter that was read to me. Apparently, it was from Jay to an organization that provided guide dogs for the blind. As told to me, the salutation, began with, Dear Head Puppy Person. Jay included a contribution check and requested the funds be used to name and train a sight dog named Edgar.

Some time had passed, and Dorothy remembers Joan placing a call to Alice Lassally. "Joan called Alice years later, we were in New York, and Alice said, 'How could you?' And Joan tried to blame it on Edgar, and Alice wasn't having any part of it."

After all this time, Dorothy still can't help but lament how many lives were affected by that memo. "It's all over and done. You can't change it. It was what it was, tragically unfortunate. After I talked to Peter and Alice, all I could think was I wish I could tell Joan. She would not believe this whole thing was bullshit. She always thought the memo was real. She was heartbroken when the memo came out. In the back of my own mind, I always thought Edgar was a part of it. I thought that he and Jay had put this together. I don't know. I just wish I could have told Joan. How things would have been different." I asked Dorothy if she thought Edgar could have gotten his hands on NBC stationery and prepared the letter himself. Dorothy doesn't think so. But that hasn't stopped pundits from wondering if Edgar engineered the whole debacle, to step out of the shadows as Joan's husband and become a full-fledged Hollywood player, an executive producer helming a show with Joan's name in the title.

On September 10, 1988, Jay was found dead in his Glendale home. He was fifty years old. *The Los Angeles Times* initially reported Jay died from unknown causes, which sent the gossip mills into overdrive. The Pasadena police report listed Jay's death as a "possible drug overdose after discovering small quantities of a substance resembling powder cocaine near his bed." Author Leslie Bennetts reported Jay died from a cocaine overdose while swimming with a male prostitute. On September 28, *The Los Angeles Times* reported the Los Angeles County Coroner's office had concluded Jay died from a heart attack. The toxicological report went on to say Jay "had ingested a low-level amount of cocaine before his death; it was not enough to kill him." And what I never knew until I read his obituary in the *LA Times* was that, in 1968, Jay won divisional honors in the US Surfing Championships at Huntington Beach. Maybe that explains why Jay was always tan.

Emily told me that NBC purchased full-page ads in show business trade publications in remembrance of Jay. She said it was the first time NBC used the graphic of an NBC Peacock with one feather missing In Memoriam for an employee. NBC had an enormous memorial/celebration of life for Jay in Studio 4. It was the kind of party Jay would have loved. Before the event, hundreds of black aloha shirts, the same star orchid pattern popularized by Tom Selleck in *Magnum, PI* were given to NBC executives, press representatives, assistants, and friends of Jay to wear in commemoration of the good times they shared with this flamboyant man. The Bombay Gin flowed, and old friends gathered not only to celebrate Jay but to say goodbye to the end of an era that will not, should not, and cannot ever be duplicated. Former Page Alan Burnett remembers Johnny Carson ending his show one evening with a tribute to Jay. Brandon Tartikoff, president of NBC Entertainment, said Michelis "Was a one-of-a-kind act. He lived his job and he was superb at it."

Chapter Twenty

HERE'S...THE TONIGHT SHOW CHAPTER

Johnny Carson was the undisputed King of Late Night television. When I began my tenure giving tours at *The Tonight Show* studio, ushering guests, and answering phones in the hallway, the show was ninety minutes long, with an estimated audience of 15.2 million viewers per night. It ran like a well-oiled machine. Johnny took over hosting duties from Jack Parr, who took them over from Steve Allen when the show originated from show New York City on October 1, 1962, and ran until Johnny bid his audience a "heartfelt goodnight" on May 22, 1992.

To the casual observer, it didn't look like Johnny began his workday until 1:15 p.m. Like clockwork, he'd drive forty miles from his clifftop home in the exclusive Point Dume beach community north of Malibu in his white Corvette with a license plate that read "360 GUY," through the midway and park in the number-one space. Why "360 GUY?" We were told it meant "All-Around Guy." Or did it? Johnny didn't seem like the kind of star who would want to draw attention to himself while driving. Anyway, it made for good Page trivia. Producers Fred de Cordova and Peter Lassally would hop into their golf cart and travel from their offices near the Page lounge to Johnny's office on the second floor above his studio. This office was where Johnny had a large picture window installed overlooking Alameda Avenue, Chadney's Restaurant, a Mexican restaurant, and a gas station.

Those of us who lead the tour groups departing at 1:00 and 1:30 made it a point to "coincidentally" be standing in the midway when Johnny arrived. Pete Hammond would invite his tour group to gather in Johnny's empty parking space and then excitedly tell them they were standing on Johnny's oil stains. It always got a laugh from the tour group, but not so much from Johnny when he arrived to work. Eba and *The Tonight Show* staff instructed us to admonish the tourists that they shouldn't approach Johnny or leave the group at any time during the tour. He was always gracious to the crowds, smiling, often waving, and sometimes saying a few words to those gathered-usually something about the tour being a rip-off. Linda Levinson had her way of dealing with her group of tourists, "I would always ask my tours if they wanted a technical tour or a gossipy tour. I never once gave a technical tour. I would take tours out to see Johnny's parking spot, and one time, Johnny pulled up in a green Rolls Royce. He rolled down the window and told the crowd, 'It's a rental.'"

It always seemed strange to me to see Johnny dressed in something other than a suit and tie. When Johnny arrived at the studio, he could often be seen in a short-sleeved knit top, mock turtleneck, or cashmere sweater, sometimes tucked into his trousers or jeans, and a light jacket. Johnny had a good physique and excellent posture, slim but not skinny looking. In an interview, Johnny said, "If I had my druthers, I'd dress like this all the time."

In 1981, Johnny acquired a new set of wheels: a first-edition DeLorean. The vehicle's uniqueness necessitated a memo to Eba from Jay Michelis, illuminating the Page staff as to what to say and what not to say about Johnny's car (best remembered as the model that blasted Michael J. Fox and Christopher Lloyd's characters *Back to the Future.)* I was told the memo said the Pages could mention Carson was an investor but not quote the MSRP of $25,000 plus tax and license. This colorful memo continued with words to the effect of, "For those adult male heterosexual members of the Guest Relations staff who are sufficiently butch to care about such things, the car has a five-speed manual transmission, a six-cylinder Renault engine, is made entirely of brushed metal and is designed to last for ten years at the very least." The Pages were also urged to tell the guests not to touch the vehicle.

The day for *The Tonight Show* staff in Burbank began at 10:00 a.m. when Johnny and Fred de Cordova would go over the headline news events that might make for good material in the monologue. Johnny would also write monologue jokes from home. Billie Freebairn-Smith, who I met when she was Eba's secretary before becoming Fred de Cordova's assistant, recalled, "Nobody on the lot saw the monologue jokes except Johnny and the writers. Each writer would turn in their monologue, and he'd choose this joke or that joke, pieces from each one." Fred and Johnny would also go over the list of guests for that evening's show. It was a challenge to book celebrities, authors, and newsmakers who had not been on other talk shows the night before. And what made for a good guest? According to an interview given by Fred de Cordova, "Somebody who had something interesting, not necessarily amusing, to say. Those are two separate things. Someone who had an interesting experience to discuss and not someone to just say they had a show opening Thursday night all over the country. It required somebody who was an interesting conversationalist." Billie said some of Johnny's favorites were "Bob Newhart, Don Rickles, James Stewart, and Tony Randall. The key to it was that somebody would do two things, amuse an audience and amuse Johnny. That's the combination we really looked for. Johnny had high regard for Steve Allen."

The Talent Coordinators would each have their specialty when it came to booking. Some went after the A-list stars, which made for a delicate juggling game. The Talent Coordinators would check the talent's availability through their personal representatives or studio publicist. With the proliferation of more late-night and daytime talk shows, *The Tonight Show* was still the first place the talent wanted to be seen. And since *The Tonight Show* gave talent their most significant exposure, no one wanted to risk losing their invitation to talk to Johnny. The coordinator also had to tell the talent if they would be the first or second guest or, heaven forbid, a third guest who could get bumped if the show ran long. Having to reschedule a guest happened more often when the show moved to a sixty-minute format in the 1980s.

I became friends with Jim McCawley, who was entrusted with finding the next breakout stand-up comic. He spent a lot of time at The Comedy Store and The Improvisation venues, watching, nurturing, waiting, and finally giving a thumbs-up to an aspiring stand-up to do their material on the show. He was the gatekeeper when it came to comics, and his only goal was to keep Johnny's comedic sensibilities in mind. Jim and I went to The Comedy Store a few times together. I was fascinated watching him watch the comics perform, one after another, for hours. When a comic finished their set, he'd get up from the table and talk to them for a few minutes with suggestions or an attaboy. Jim rooted for comics to succeed, and he would hear their same jokes and observations repeatedly until they were polished to perfection. It could be a stressful job that often kept him out into the early morning hours with comics hounding him, some thinking he was an asshole for not putting them on the show. Jim's reputation and job were on the line every time Johnny introduced a comic who went through that center curtain to perform. Stand-up comedian and comedy historian Rich Shydner, who appeared on *The Tonight Show* about a dozen times, summed up the key to Jim's twenty-five-year-long stint with Johnny: "Jim knew the difference between nightclub-funny and TV-funny."

The Talent Coordinators would have to pre-interview each guest, to construct the segment with questions and answers, and to prep Johnny. The guests' stories had to be concise, maybe amusing, definitely interesting. Fred would also let Johnny know if a comedy sketch that evening would include one of his signature characters, from Floyd R Turbo to Art Fern to Tarzan. When I was there, the comedy sketches were rehearsed but always taped before a live audience as part of the regular show. It was fun to see Johnny away from his desk working through a bit like *"Tea Time Matinee."* He looked like he enjoyed the process, refining the jokes up until the last minute.

The average tour lasted one hour, and you could kill a good twenty minutes once you got your group inside Studio 1. This was the home of *The Tonight Show* ever since the show moved from New York to Burbank on May 1, 1972. The studio was built in 1952 and was first used for *All-Star Review*, which featured a different host each week during its run.

As an audience member, one drawback when seeing a TV show taped is the large cameras on the stage floor that could often block a good view of the entertainers. Bob Hope's idea was to make a permanent audience seating area with a steep incline. Several times throughout the year, we'd be able to tell guests they had a special treat at the end of *The Tonight Show*. The scenery department would scurry about and quickly reset the area in the center of the stage where Johnny did his monologue so Bob Hope could tape a segment for one of his numerous specials. A few days before his special aired, Bob would simply stand in front of a camera against an unremarkable curtain and read from a ginormous stack of cue cards with printing on them so large astronauts could read them from space. He'd read about twenty minutes worth of jokes that would be edited down to about five minutes of airable material, with a generous amount of fake laughs added for good measure. In the early days of Monty Hall's version of *Let's Make a Deal*, he taped in Studio 1, and when Johnny and Bob weren't using the studio on the weekends, other game shows would tape there, too. The studio had a seating capacity of 475, which Johnny always filled. If the audience didn't occupy every seat, the stagehands could draw a curtain, blocking the empty seats from the guest host's (and the camera's) view.

When they entered the studio, the first thing our tour group noticed was how small the set looked. And, without all the lights on, the scenery seemed kind of drab. We'd remind our guests that they were looking at the stage sets for the first time in 3-D, which is cool and all, but a camera only captures a 2-D image. The Art Department designed this illusion purposely to look good on television, including the backdrop behind Johnny's desk. While it looked like a panoramic view of a dazzling skyline, it was merely a painted backdrop. Seasonally, the scenery would change to reflect the holiday season: Easter Lillies in the Spring, Poinsettias in December. The second thing you'd notice was that it was always, extremely cold in the studio. Yes, the lights in the studio could warm the place up quickly, but Johnny's prevailing thought was that by keeping the audience cold, it would keep them alert. A warm studio could make an audience lethargic. Sitcoms copied this model, including the talk shows hosted by David Letterman.

At no time were the members of the tour allowed on the set. Pages were told to NEVER sit behind Johnny's desk. That didn't stop Courtney

Conte, Sandy Crompton, or Tommy Patino. Others have written about what was underneath Johnny's desk. Writer Bill Zehme reported Johnny kept a tattered rubber chicken and a wood arrow from an infamous Custard sketch that went wrong. The chicken symbolized comedy, the arrow failure. But Tommy told me he also saw an ashtray and a fan under the desk, installed to disperse all evidence of Johnny taking a few puffs during the commercial breaks. He also that noticed Johnny's chair was slightly higher than his guests. Tommy also managed to steal one of the coveted double-headed pencils Johnny would flip between his fingers and tap on his desk during the commercial breaks. Tommy sent me a picture of the white pencil with *The Tonight Show* embossed in black lettering. I asked him which of his children or grandchildren chewed on the pencil. He said, "Those marks were made by Johnny when he was drumming on his desk."

Our job was to give the tourists a little backstage gossip they couldn't ordinarily find in the tabloids. We'd tell a story about a Suzanne Somers appearance on the show that was always good for a laugh (or a groan). Suzanne had come up with a bit to show Johnny some relaxation techniques using food. She put cucumber slices on his eyes and had him put his feet in a large bowl of Jell-O. It wasn't rocket science, but it made for good television. Once the bit was over, the food was taken backstage and set on a table next to the prop storage area that Propmaster Jack Grant manned. No sooner had the show ended than the cucumbers and Jello-O had been eaten! This story, perhaps apocryphal, was told for years during the studio tour. True or not, one of the rules of show biz is never to eat prop food (or any food backstage) unless it is on the Craft Services table.

During the nightly taping, Fred de Cordova would be seated next to a large clock just off-stage to Johnny's right. Fred would hold up a cue card or make a hand gesture to break for a commercial or stretch for time. Once they were clear, meaning the camera was no longer taping them, a phalanx of producers, talent coordinators, and hair and make-up artists descended on Johnny with the precision of a NASCAR pit crew. Johnny would remain seated at his desk, usually smoking, while he was briefed on the upcoming segment, or a decision was made about how long the forthcoming interview would run, or if Johnny had a concern, it could be addressed. If a guest got bumped and asked to return on another evening, they would still get paid their union scale fee for their appearance, or lack of appearance.

Then there was the time Johnny was chatting with Angie Dickinson. When they went to the commercial break, quite by surprise, Angie's hair and make-up person popped up from behind the couch, where she had been lying out of camera view throughout the segment, to touch up her look.

Our Page manual included tidbits we'd sprinkle through the tour. We boasted that Johnny was the highest-paid entertainer on television. He also had logged the most hours of television exposure, over 3,000, when I got there. Eventually, he reached a total of 6,714 programs, a number that included ninety-minute and sixty-minute shows. According to the *Guinness Book of World Records*, Johnny's record has been surpassed by Regis Philbin. In an interview, Johnny confessed to Regis that he got nervous every night before stepping through the peacock curtain. "You get out and find out how the audience is going to react. I think you need that little edge to stand back and see if they are a little up or down that night." The Regis/Johnny behind-the-scenes segment was the brainchild of former NBC Page Tom Chasuk, who,along with Peter Lassally, made it all happen.

Johnny's announcer and sidekick, Ed McMahon, would arrive at the studio via limousine, but we wouldn't see him until the audience warm-up. With his signature hardy "Hi-Yo," Ed's booming voice welcomed the eager crowd. We all had to listen to him tell the same jokes for years, most of them involving booze, like when he'd ask the audience if they got the "free margaritas they were supposed to get while waiting in line." Not a funny joke during the summer when it would be 110 degrees in the shade. He would also point out the applause sign, then take his place behind his announcer podium as the band struck up the theme song. He'd announce the guests, then say those two words everyone in the audience was waiting to hear: "Here's Johnny." Occasionally, Ed would have to re-record the opening announcement if the show ran out of time, excluding the guest's name that got bumped.

Ed was a terrific sidekick. He gave Johnny plenty of material on which to comment, from Ed's drinking habits to his Alpo dog food commercials. Ed would also announce sketches for Johnny, sometimes with "*The Mighty Carson Art Players,*" whose name was both an homage to and a rip-off of humorist and radio personality Fred Allen's "*Mighty Allen Art Players.*" I never saw Johnny and Ed rehearse a "*Carnac, The Magnificent*" sketch. Johnny didn't rehearse his monologue on the stage, either. By 5:15 p.m., Johnny left his office, descended the stairs, got a quick make-up touch-up, finished his cigarette, and walked to his place backstage. There, he waited to hear Ed's signature catchphrase., "Here's Johnny!" One of the stage managers, often Irv Davis, would open the Peacock Curtain, allowing Johnny to make his effortless entrance. Once he walked through the multicolored curtain, Johnny could read his cue cards, which had been attached to a custom wooden wall just below the cameras. It wasn't necessary to write the entire joke verbatim on the cards. Johnny was well familiar with the material by the time he took center stage and only needed to see keywords or phrases to make America laugh.

"The NBC Orchestra," as it was officially billed, but better known as "The Tonight Show Band," had its own pre-show schedule. Once the giant elephant doors were closed at 2:00 p.m., the seventeen-member band, led by the sartorially splendid Doc Severinsen, would begin rehearsing for about an hour. They would run through about six of the over one thousand charts on file, customizing the music for each guest. Fun fact: Doc's first name is Carl. The band would then rehearse with the evening's musical guest. Dropping in on the rehearsals was a Page perk. On my salary, I could never have afforded tickets to see the various artists performing on the show. I saw everyone from Liberace to Tony Bennett, extraordinary drummers Buddy Rich and Louie Bellson, opera stars Beverly Sills, Placido Domingo, and Luciano Pavarotti, violinist Itzhak Perlman, singers Steve Lawrence and Eydie Gormé, and Dolly Parton. While the rehearsal took place, the tour group could hear the music and maybe see a guest arrive.

If Doc were off for the night or filling in for Ed McMahon, Tommy Newsom (with a seemingly bland personality but a lot of talent) would lead the band. And when he was unavailable, Assistant Musical Director Shelly Cohen got the gig. Johnny nicknamed Shelly "The Kosher Mantovani." Besides Ed McMahon, Shelly was the only other staff member to have worked with Johnny throughout his show's entire run. Another Fun Fact: I went to Agoura High School with Steven, Shelly's son. Johnny's son Cory lived with the Cohens for a while when they moved the show to California. Cory was an excellent musician. When most of us were trying to learn the guitar lick at the beginning of The Standell's "*Dirty Water,*" Cory played complicated classical pieces. Cory and I became friends, and a few years later, he moved into the same apartment building I was living in on Avon Street, within walking distance from the studio. Cory and I would stroll through the neighborhood, and I remember him picking a few figs off a tree, opening them, and showing me how to eat them properly. He was a real-life Euell Gibbons!

On a few occasions, The Pages would have a brush with greatness with a guest before the show began. Renee had a great idea I wish I had thought of. She purchased Sophia Loren's autobiography and had her autograph it when she was a guest on the show. When Tommy Patino was working the show, he greeted screen legend, Ginger Rogers, at her limousine and carried her garment bag, hanging it in her dressing room. Tommy smilingly recalled, "She said, 'Come here, young man,' and she gave me the biggest hug. She thanked me and called me a dear. I'll never forget that!"

Once the show started, it got pretty boring back in the hallway. I saw a well-dressed man with a cane standing outside a dressing room. He looked exhausted. I asked if I could get him a chair, but he just leaned against the two-tone beige and brown wall, lamenting he had to take his client to Disneyland after her appearance on the show. I asked, and he told me his client was Kristy McNichol, best remembered for the TV shows *Family* and *Empty Nest*. He explained, "She wants to go on the new attraction, Splash Mountain." I asked if he'd called ahead to make some VIP arrangements to whisk Kristy in and out of the park without waiting in lines-and since he had a cane, could they get a golf cart for him? I felt sorry for the poor schlub and asked if I could make a few calls on his behalf. I'd never called Disneyland, but I was bored and figured, what the heck? I've got nothing to lose. So, I got their Head of Security on the phone and warned them a mob could gather when they saw Kristy, and it would be in their best interest to provide VIP service to her. I was given a name for the man to call when he arrived. I ripped a pink piece of paper off the ever-present message pad with complete instructions and handed them to the man with the cane, who was astonished at the initiative I took on his behalf. He gave me his card and said he would send me a bottle of Dom Perignon Champagne. The name on the card was Jay Bernstein. He was a powerful manager whose future clients included Farrah Fawcett, Linda Evans, and Suzanne Somers. He was no schlub.

A decade later, I was broke and out of work due to a Writers Guild strike. I called the number on Jay's card and told his assistant, humorously, that he owed me a bottle of Dom Perignon and that he should contact me. We met two days later, and Jay couldn't have been nicer. Over lunch at the "in" restaurant, Ma Maison, Jay offered me a job as his Head of Development for his production company. It was a stressful job that lasted nine long months. Jay was a yeller and one of those bosses who thought nothing of calling my home at 3:00 a.m., ranting about some frustrations he had. Oh, and that cane? It was an affectation that housed a sword and, on occasion, drugs. Before I quit the job to work on a TV series, he presented me with a bottle of Dom. By this point, I had more than earned it.

I will confess to being a bit of a naughty girl in a dressing room. When *The Tonight Show's* format was ninety minutes long, my former boyfriend, still a close and beloved friend, occasionally appeared as a guest. This segment was often reserved for authors, magicians, raconteurs, or people who demonstrated products or gadgets or shared fun science experiments with Johnny. When both of us were in-between relationships, I'd knock on his dressing room door, and we'd fool around. We'd stop to watch the monologue then we'd get busy again during the commercial break. It was fun, kind of thrilling, a bit dangerous, and exhilarating! Thankfully, Bob Dolce, the Talent Coordinator assigned to my friend, never caught us. After the taping, we'd grab some dinner, go back to his place and watch the show later that same night. We both giggled as I pointed out the subtle smile on his face following our romp while he spoke with Johnny.

In addition to seating the audience, we were responsible for keeping our eye on them during the show's taping. If an audience member said something like "How hot was it?" when Johnny tried to elicit a crowd response, that was okay. If someone started to heckle Johnny, we would immediately escort them out of the studio. The ever-dutiful Page Tom Chasuk did kick someone out of the audience. When Johnny completed his monologue, the extracted guy's friends yelled in unison to Johnny, pointing at Tom, and pleading with Johnny to let their friend back in. Johnny said, "Let him back in." Tom was so mad, "I was thinking it was his frickin' rule and I was just doing what we were suppose to do. What was Johnny going to say? He had no choice but for me to bring the guy back to his seat."

I didn't see many of Johnny's monologues because The Pages were told we should turn our backs to the stage and watch the crowd to see if anyone had a weapon. Many years later, visitors were required to pass through NBC's metal detectors, much like the ones in airports. I hope the ones at the airport work more consistently than ours did.

During the commercial breaks, we were to walk to the front row of the audience area and block anyone from trying to get on the stage. One evening (thankfully, I wasn't there), an audience member got past a Page and on to the stage. Irv Davis, the man behind the Peacock Curtain, helped tackle the guy. Stage Manager Kevin Quinn, the son of the show's director, Bobby Quinn, rushed to protect Johnny and grabbed for the intruder but slipped. A few weeks later, Kevin told me he vowed never to wear his Gucci shoes on the slippery tile floor again and would only wear sneakers from then on. Fortunately, the security guards whisked the fan away.

The Pages rarely got on camera, but when a guest dropped out at the last minute, *The Tonight Show* staff notified us that Johnny would be doing an audience participation bit titled *"Stump the Band."* Here's how it worked: a Talent Coordinator would talk to guests lined up to see the show and find about a dozen eager volunteers who knew some wacky, obscure song. Johnny would then select an audience member and ask for the title of a song. It was Ed, Doc, and The Band's job to try to play the correct music for the song title. The band did some silly schtick, and Johnny asked the guest if the band was right, and if not, the audience member would sing a little bit of the song. Afterward, a Page would hand Johnny an envelope that contained a gift certificate for dinner, or an event in the Los Angeles area, to thank the guest for their effort. So, how was the Page picked for that evening's *"Stump the Band?"* It was simply based on who had seniority on the crew assigned to the show that evening.

When I was informed it was my "Stump the Band" night, I felt like I had won the lottery! I had seniority, but it meant my dear friend, Dinah Brein, wouldn't get to do it. To this day, I still feel bad because she left the staff before she ever had an opportunity to be selected. Plus, I wasn't wearing closed-toed shoes! What if I got busted and was sent to Eba's office for this unconscionable fashion infraction? The time came, and one of the stage managers took me to the make-up room, where I was seated next to Ed as we both had our faces powdered by Harry Blake. I'd seen his name for years on the credits of *The Tonight Show, Laugh-In,* and just about every variety show shot in Burbank, so I was excited he was taking the shine off my twenty-two-year-old complexion. After the monologue, I was escorted by one of the stage managers to the audience section, where Johnny interviewed the singing audience members. I was directed to stand two steps above Johnny and hand him an envelope when he turned and extended his hand. I was not to speak to Johnny, but it was okay to laugh at his jokes. As the lights came up after the commercial, I caught a glimpse of myself in the monitor on stage and weaseled my way on camera so my family and friends could clearly see me. And just like that, it was all over. Johnny thanked me for my expert envelope giving, and as soon as the taping concluded, I ran to the Page lounge and called everybody I could think of to watch the show that night.

Courtney Conte was able to do *"Stump the Band"* twice, but one time stood out more than the other. "There were two women out in the audience who were quite tall and well endowed, and of course, Bobby Quinn told Johnny (to pick) those two. The two girls stood up, and they looked like they were showgirls from Vegas. Johnny asked if they had a song and all of a sudden, Ed and Doc were extremely interested because these two women were beautiful. Johnny played up the moment, and when they were finished singing, Johnny turned to me and asked, 'What do we have for you tonight?' Meanwhile, I was going through the envelopes with the usual gift certificates, Chadney's, The Smoke House, and then I spotted a Goodyear Blimp ride." Courtney continued, "I pulled that envelope out, and Johnny looked at me and smiled. I gave him a big fucking joke, and he never forgot that. He was always nice to me and talked to me. I was friends with (his late son) Ricky. Johnny didn't talk to too many people."

Not every Page wanted to hand an envelope to Johnny. Linda Levinson, a confident brunette, was known for her quick wit, radiant smile, and generous bosom. Ultimately, she was shy when it came to being on camera. Comedy writing was her focus. Linda says she was asked several times to do *"Stump the Band"* and always deflected, jokingly suggesting she'd do it when NBC could find a blazer she could close.

When I started working on the show, Monday nights were dedicated to a revolving door of guest hosts. Often I would see David Brenner, John Davidson, and McLean Stevenson hosting. One night, Irv Davis gave Steve Martin the keys to his Porsche, and he used it to make an entrance. As Fred de Cordova's assistant, Billie saw a lot of guest hosts come and go. "Not everybody was good at it. We made a few mistakes. A good guest didn't always make a good guest host. Occasionally, we'd luck out and get a comic like George Carlin or Steve Martin. They did their homework and came prepared with new jokes in their own voice for the monologue."

And sometimes, I'd get to see a man I idolized, Steve Allen, behind the desk. It was like nostalgia came alive! Before Joan Rivers, it seemed the only women who got a shot at the guest host chair were singers like Diana Ross, Beverly Sills, and Helen Reddy.

Tom Hansen and Gregg Moscoe remembered Joey Bishop's guest-hosting stints. They both had completely different experiences. Tom recalled how Joey went into the audience to do a bit. "He grabbed me by the hand and put his arm around me. All of a sudden, he made me part of the deal. He asked me a question about how many tickets were in the envelope. I said, I believe four, and he said, come over here, I can't hear you. He played off of me." Gregg can never forget his experience with the guest host: "Joey was up in the audience doing a talent hunt. I was standing next to him with the giveaway goodies. He held the mic out in front of a woman who was singing, and she grabbed the mic away from him. He stood back did a shrug take to the cameras. And then he turned around and smacked me, open hand slap to the face. As I stood there, momentarily stunned, I weighed the choice of standing there smiling or smacking him back."

One night I'll never forget. It was on October 3, 1979. Richard Dawson was the guest host. Singer Della Reese, the first Black female to guest host the show, was the musical entertainment that evening. While singing *"Pieces of Dreams,"* she suddenly fell to the ground. The sound was loud. Immediately, I could tell something was horribly wrong. She was having a convulsion. Richard and Doc ran to her side, and soon, a doctor from the audience joined them. As I recall, the stagehands lowered the curtain to protect Della's privacy. The taping was halted, and the Pages were instructed to usher the audience out of the studio. A rerun aired that evening. Della said in an interview, "I never lost consciousness, but I wasn't in control." Attendants who carried her to an ambulance heard her pleading, "Lord, help me. God, help me." Della had suffered a near-fatal massive hemorrhagic stroke a result of an aneurysm her brain. Following two surgeries, she thankfully made a full recovery.

The guest host that caused numerous problems, even back in 1976, was Bill Cosby. In retrospect, it was so apparent that he was one man backstage and another in front of an audience. My Page pal Cindy Hain, whose father Ed was a security guard at the show, remembers when Cosby arrived with a large entourage. "He was moving down the hallway, so I plastered myself against the wall to let them pass. Bill Cosby shoulder-checked me as he went by. I never gave it a thought until recently. He also 'fell' on me once."

I saw a pattern in the Pages that were assigned to work the show when Cosby guest hosted. Balling up my feminist fists, I asked to see Eba Hawkins. I marched into her office and point-blank asked her why only the male Pages worked those shows. Eba shook it off and said that Mr. Cosby requested only male Pages, and that's what they had to do. Tom Hansen worked as the CB Page in charge in the hallway numerous times. He said Eba told him (now remember, this was back in the mid-seventies) that a female Page should never be alone in a room with Cosby. Tom also recalled a show Cosby hosted where he was "talking about something pertaining to the Tampa Bay Buccaneers. I worked it, and it appeared Mr. Cosby was drunk or high on something. It didn't look like the same show I watched from home that night. It was heavily edited," he said.

The Pages weren't the only staffers who witnessed Cosby's predatory prowess. Whenever there was a guest host, staff members from *The Tonight Show*, often the people who handled the fan mail, were assigned to prepare the guest host's dressing room. The task involved ensuring the dressing rooms were clean and stocked with any particular food or beverages requested for the evening, as well as sitting with the guest host in case there were any last-minute needs. Two different young women came back to *The Tonight Show* offices and reported that Cosby was constantly walking around the dressing room with his dick hanging out. After that, a male who worked in the office was sent to tend to Cosby's dressing room, and he complained, as well. According to my source, this behavior never happened with the other guest hosts, "Just Cosby."

And then there was the time Cosby offered to "mentor" one of the young Asian female Pages. Excitedly, she told two male Pages that Cosby wanted to "help her." He said he was going to San Francisco, that she should come with him, and that he would get her a separate room. It would all be platonic. The two male pages said an emphatic "no" to her. Renee echoed my exact sentiments when she said, "Imagine a star like that hitting on the lowest rung in terms of an entry-level job."

I found it amusing that many decades later, Courtney, who had been an Executive for Carsey-Werner Productions, the company behind *The Cosby Show,* continued his mischievous ways. While Cosby was incarcerated, having been convicted of sexual assault (a decision that was overturned), Courtney sent him a braille Playboy magazine. "I found it online. I sent it anonymously."

Securing a job on *The Tonight Show* directly from the Page staff wasn't likely but also wasn't impossible. Onetime Page Debbie Vickers got a break working on the show and rose through the ranks to become Executive Producer of *The Tonight Show with Jay Leno.* But in other cases, nepotism wasn't always the golden ticket to the inner circle of *The Tonight Show.* Marilee's father, Jim Mahoney, was a well-respected publicist for A-list stars. Marilee had access to Hollywood royalty: everybody from Frank Sinatra to Jack Lemmon to Gene Kelly. On weekends, she would accompany her dad to his private golf club, and there she met Fred de Cordova. She had more than a passing acquaintance with him, and when she was recovering from foot surgery, Fred even let her use his beloved golf cart, the one he used to travel from *The Tonight Show* bungalow to Studio 1. So, when an internship to take notes in The Green Room, the holding area for guests and their guests during *The Tonight Show* pre-production meetings, became available, Marilee thought it would be a perfect fit. She reached out to another longtime family friend, talent executive extraordinaire David Tebet, who recommended her to Fred for the gig. Turns out she didn't get the assignment. Marilee went into Eba's office, sobbing. Eba asked what kind of problem she had with Fred. She had no problem with him, but Fred had a problem with Marilee. Fred didn't want Marilee to overhear him or his staff saying anything bad about her father's clients in the meeting. Fred was concerned Marilee wouldn't be able to keep the people and topics discussed confidential from her father, and he wouldn't feel as free to talk in her presence. The irony is, Marilee had been privy to a lot of private information over the years, the kind of information she could have sold to the tabloids, but she never did. She would have been the perfect person to keep Fred's behind-the-scenes secrets. Marilee went to another family acquaintance, John McMahon, the then-President of the network, and he consoled her by saying, "Not getting that job was the best thing that happened. You don't want to take this a step further. Fred is a powerful man and not a nice man. Something better for you is down the pike."

When I heard Eba's former secretary, Billie, got the position as Fred's assistant, I was thrilled for her. It was the perfect prestigious job for Billie, a single mother who appreciated the steady job with regular hours. I never suspected that during the first two years she worked with Fred, she was "scared" and "intimated" by him. Billie shared her discomfort with another female co-worker who told her not to be scared because "No one listens to Fred." Billie felt she could say whatever she needed from that moment on. Her relationship improved so much that she had no qualms about pitching in and helped type Fred's autobiography during her downtime.

A female Page told me she turned down a proposition from *Tonight Show* Director Bobby Quinn, even though he carefully explained he and his wife had "an understanding." Another Page told me Bobby had nine children when she began a fling with him. (Kevin Quinn, Bobby's son, mentioned he was one of seven children when he was interviewed on Mark Malkoff's *Carsonpodcast*.) She says they had a great time until one evening when he left her apartment and was shocked to see his red Porsche had been stolen. Less than twenty-four hours after the car went missing, the *National Enquirer* called her. I'm guessing they got her address from the police report. When the *National Enquirer* reporter phoned her to ask what she knew, she calmly replied, "You must have the wrong person. I don't know who that is."

On Monday, May 26, 2014, a small group of Pages, about ten of us, went on our own final, self-guided private tour of the facility. NBC had sold the facility, and we wanted to take one last lap around the plant before no one would be able to let us in again. We went to Studio 1, long emptied, then proceeded downstairs to what was known as The Subterranean Lounge, located at the end of the downstairs hallway. When we occupied the space, it looked like a locker room (minus the showers). Each Page had a locker so they could change from their street clothes into their uniforms and also have a place to stash their personal belongings. We'd have our pre-production meeting for *The Tonight Show* there before greeting the public. Tommy Patino vaguely recalled sleeping in there one night when, in his words, he "got shitfaced at Pepe's (restaurant)." He went on to explain, "I used to drive in from Long Beach, and I woke up Saturday morning to the sound of (the game show) *High Rollers* (blaring) from the speaker in the room going on in Studio 3."

The door was locked, but we found a maintenance man who opened it for us. Much to our shock, the lounge had been completely transformed. Our lockers had been replaced by walls lined with mirrors. The maintenance man told us the space was later converted for Jay Leno to use as a gym. But before that, he told us, it had been converted into a private area for Johnny Carson, complete with a shower and vanity. *The Tonight Show* staff renamed our lounge The Escape Room. NBC had become more and more concerned about Johnny's safety and was determined he needed to have a secret, quick escape route in case of danger. So, a door was installed that gave Johnny access to an underground tunnel that led from his Escape Room to the Administration Building. Most everyone who worked at NBC Burbank knew about this not-so-secret tunnel. We used it to keep out of the rain when crossing from the midway area to the Administration building where the Hungry Peacock Commissary was located.

On May 22, 1992, Johnny had his 4530th and final show, viewed by over fifty million people. Johnny and his wife, Alexis exited the building through the secret tunnel. A waiting helicopter took them to their Malibu home, where they greeted a roster of invitation-only guests that included *The Tonight Show* staff and family, who drank and danced the night away to the sounds of Les Brown and his Band of Renown.

When Johnny received his final standing ovation as host of *The Tonight Show,* the last song Doc and the band played was *"I'll Be Seeing You."* All that remains now is the charming area across the street from the former NBC Burbank facility, the Johnny Carson Park, located at 400 Bob Hope Dr., Burbank, CA 91505. It is dedicated to the man who was America's Nightlight. For twenty-nine years, six months, and three weeks, Johnny was our touchstone, an intelligent entertainer with a calming, familiar voice in the middle of the night who let us know that despite wars, assassinations, and the continuing changing social and political landscape, everything was going to be okay.

Chapter Twenty-One

WE CAN'T GO HOME AGAIN

When asked what it was like to be a Page at NBC, the answer usually involves the phrase, "It was like a fraternity or sorority." Many of the Pages became roommates because let's face it, we weren't earning a living wage. By the time I left the staff, I was making $2.25 an hour, and my rent was $225 a month. The workplace was frantic at times. We all tried to cover for each other if someone was sick or when extra Pages were needed to work a show. It was also extremely competitive. We were given only a year and a half to find a job, or we'd be asked to leave the Page program. Few of the Pages stayed with NBC for their entire career. But many of us have stayed in touch, long after we hung up our polyester uniforms.

Getting a job off the Page staff wasn't a slam dunk. As much as we networked with people, it wasn't easy to stay under the wing of the Peacock. A few Pages I knew left against their will before the eighteen months were up. After calling Eba Hawkins weekly for nearly two and a half years, Neil Weiner was offered a Page job the day after he graduated from USC. At the time, it was the best day of his life. Neil, an affable guy looking to work his way up the ladder, was pulled aside after a few months and was told, "This job's not for you. You're not corporate material." Thankfully, Neil was always and will always be a great schmoozer, and he was accepted into the William Morris Agent Training Program before starting a sales career. Neil and *CPO Sharkey* co-star Peter Isacksen owned a post-production facility, Postmark Video Services and Video Events. Now he works with the top producers in town in need of production facilities.

Linda (Levinson) Taylor also briefly worked for The William Morris Agency but got burnt out on show business. She married and moved far away from LA. She became both a mom and a force to be reckoned with! Linda also had a stint as a broadcaster while working in public relations.

One Page never learned his lesson and got booted twice from two jobs for the same infraction: saying something terrible about a celebrity. When he worked at Universal City Studio, someone asked him about the height of actor Robert Conrad, best remembered as James West on the TV series *The Wild, Wild West*. He said something about him being short. Sure enough, someone on his tour (probably the man who asked the question) reported the remark back to Conrad, who had the Tour Guide fired. When this same guide came to work at NBC as a Page, he made a comment linking Frank Sinatra to the Mafia. He said something to the effect of "Frank Sinatra is guesting on *The Tonight Show* this evening. And, he's invited some of his friends like Lucky and Bugsy to join him." As the story goes, Frank called Jay Michelis personally and said, "Do you consider me your friend. Get rid of that Page." You guessed it; he was asked to leave immediately. Another rule of Pagedom: Never disrespect the talent.

Another Page, who had his sights set on becoming a writer, was too creative when it came to writing. He was let go when a story appeared in one of the trade papers (*Variety* or *The Hollywood Reporter)* announcing he'd sold a script to NBC. The details of how he did this are kind of sketchy, but it may have involved him writing this press release on official NBC stationery he had stolen.

The saddest was when Lesa (Lindsay) Mattingly lost her job. A group of people lined up at the wrong end of the entrance gate. Lesa went over to the group to remedy the situation. A film crew from *The Today Show* was doing a feature story on the breaking news that Fred Silverman was just appointed the network's new president. Someone from their staff put a camera and microphone in front of Lesa and asked her if she'd like to ask Fred Silverman a question. Lesa humorously said, "Could he give us a raise?" A couple waiting in line overheard the flippant remark and wrote a letter to Fred Silverman that was forwarded to Eba. Lesa was immediately summoned to Eba's office. He wanted to fire her on the spot, but Lesa asked for-and was allowed-two weeks before she left so she could find another job and say her goodbyes.

Lesa had lost her dream job. She was devastated. Her off-the-cuff remark violated some policies about Pages always giving the public a good impression. Luckily, she got to go out in style because on her last evening as an NBC employee, Lesa was picked to be the Page who gave the envelopes to Johnny Carson during the show's *"Stump the Band"* segment.

Lesa and I were so excited! She called her family in Kentucky and told them to be on the lookout for her that evening. Lesa was visibly nervous, but I told her not to worry because I'd have her back. As Johnny made his way up and down the aisle, Lesa stood in the audience on the stairs. I made sure I stood off-camera, to the side of the stage, to have a clear view of Lesa on the in-studio monitor. I would give her hand signals to move to the left or the right, so her face could be seen between Johnny and the audience member. She looked radiant! It almost went off without a hitch.

Days later, Lesa is now working as a waitress at Los Caballos, a Mexican restaurant near the studio. As luck would have it, Eba and her friends were seated at Lesa's station. Eba was startled to see Lesa and told her she'd gotten her in trouble again with NBC brass. Lesa wondered why, as she was no longer a Page. Wouldn't you know: the people who complained about Lesa were told she had been fired. That was true. So imagine their surprise when they saw her handing envelopes to Johnny during *"Stump the Band."* Lesa moved back to her hometown, owned a dress store, married, became Mom to Elizabeth Grace, happily divorced, and worked for the Head Start project before retiring to become a full-time Nana to Charli Rose.

My Page pals often wondered what it would be like to return to 3000 W. Alameda one more time. So, a group of us did that before the NBC Burbank facility was sold to Warner Brothers in 2015 as part of a massive expansion plan. The Pages, about forty of us, gathered in the tour lobby waiting. And just like riding a bike, the tour spiel came pouring out of our mouths as we took one more lap around the stages. Blake Jones, the son of Pages Renee Palyo and Tim Jones, joined us on the final tour. I immediately knew Renee and Tim did a good job parenting their thirteen-year-old when, without prompting from his parents, he politely offered to take a picture of all of us old folks standing in front of the current NBC logo.

Sometimes, I won't see a Page for years, even decades, and we pick right back up where we left off. I met Courtney Conte at his office, where I saw that he did get to live his dream of becoming a mogul. He left the Page staff and went to work for the NBC TV series *Real People*. I was in Courtney's office when his dear friend, *Laugh-In* and *Real People* executive producer George Schlatter, reminded us via phone that he nicknamed Courtney "The Wrinkle King" because of his fondness for dating older actresses. George went on to say Courtney prematurely had personalized luggage tags made for himself that read "Producer." He used the tags to attract the attention of the ladies and in a way, set himself on a path that would lead to his dream. As Pages, Courtney, and I ate, drank, and studied all things NBC. Case in point; Courtney dressed as Fred Silverman, and I dressed as the NBC Peacock at Cris Neel's Halloween party. Courtney has fulfilled his dream, serving as an executive for numerous production companies. And during our chat, Courtney had one more memory that involved me!

In late 1989, I ran into Courtney in Studio 3 at NBC. We were both working on a game show pilot. Courtney produced the pilot for WB/Telepictures. My friend Fred Wostbrock hired me to be a Rehearsal Contestant, and before you get too excited, I couldn't win any money. I played the game repeatedly, enabling the host and crew to rehearse their cues and dialogue, saving time once the pilot began taping. It was a simple concept based on a popular game, but instead of filling in the squares under the word BINGO, the name used was, TRUMP. Yes, The Donald, his then-wife Ivana affectionately called him, even dabbled in the game show biz. The show was titled *Trump Card*.

The Donald was best known as a celebrated New York Real Estate Entrepreneur and Atlantic City casino owner at the time. His most significant claims to fame were restoring Central Park's iconic Wollman

Rink for ice skaters and slapping his name on buildings. I'd seen photos of The Donald and his wife in publications, so when we were told Trump would appear on the pilot, we were all curious to check out who this big shot from New York was. And, boy, I sure found out who he was—fast!

The Donald arrived with a small entourage, including a beautiful blonde with a dazzling smile and long flowing hair. I'm thinking: The Donald has a hot, doting assistant; good for him. A few moments later, we were all told to stop what we were doing and gather so The Donald could give us a congratulatory pep talk before the taping. I was seated behind The Donald, and I vividly remember what happened next. The Donald, with one hand, one tiny little hand, a small palm with Vienna sausage-like fingers, gesturing wildly, marveled at the splendor of the set and commended us on all our hard work. The other tiny hand was on the blonde's ass. Fred and I started giggling like schoolgirls about how crass his pork-filled fingers looked while grabbing the blonde's behind.

I saw Courtney at a small Page get-together in Westwood, CA, decades later. He told me, and this was before The Donald became The 45th President of the United States, what went on behind the scenes at the *Trump Card* taping after I had left. It turns out Ivana arrived unexpectedly at NBC and was on her way over to the stage! Courtney, ever the problem solver, grabbed the blonde and hid her in the plush office of an NBC executive, far, far away from the prying eyes of The Mrs. If it hadn't been for Courtney's quick thinking, the current Mrs. Trump would have met the future Mrs. Trump, Marla Maples.

Our platonic Page friendships have spanned continents. Pete and Roxanne were touring a rainy, foggy Venice, Italy, standing on the Bridge of Sighs, when they heard a familiar voice. In unison, they said, "Chris Gallagher," and indeed, it was she! Roxanne, Dinah, Tim, and Brian also did a quickie tour of Europe. Roxanne and Brian later jetted off to Hong Kong and Tokyo. Cindy Hain worked for Princess Tours and secured a free twenty-one-day Mediterranean cruise for us. The first stop was Rome, where we ran into Tony Cacciotti, an actor I knew from *The Gong*

Show. He and his wife, Valerie Harper, had just shot an episode on board the Pacific Princess, AKA *The Love Boat*. We were meeting the same ship in Naples in a few days. But first, we wanted to tour Rome. Tony and Valerie were traveling with a cute, young, blond guy. We asked them all if they wanted to hop in a cab with us as we were on our way to see The Vatican. Tony and Valerie were too tired, but the cute blond guy checked with them, and they said he should go with Cindy and me.

At this point, I assumed the young man was their personal assistant, so I paid for the cab, his ticket to the Sistine Chapel, and all our food and beverages. We took a few photos together, and I wanted to make sure he received them once we returned from our trip. He said, "Send them to ABC. I'll get them." Made sense to me. *The Love Boat* was an ABC show. Perhaps he was hired by the network to work with Tony and Valerie? When I got home, I showed my vacation photos to a few friends. When they saw the cute blond guy, they shrieked, "That's Grant Show!" He was, at the time, the heartthrob on the ABC daytime drama *Ryan's Hope*, where he played Rick Hyde. He later achieved primetime fame as Jake Hanson on *Beverly Hills, 90210, Melrose Place, and Models, Inc.* Years later, at a Writers Guild Award Show, I ran into Grant, who recalled our Vatican Vay-cay with great delight. I had an opportunity to flaunt my ignorance when Grant couldn't get over the fact I didn't know he was an actor.

Roxanne (Yamaguchi) Moster's Page background came in handy when she transitioned to a career as the Director of Media Relations for UCLA Health Sciences, interacting with local and international media representatives. She presented heartwarming stories to media outlets, including a project we worked on for Operation: Mend, which provides reconstructive surgery to wounded veterans, and mental health support to them and their families. She was also responsible for dealing with the media when high-profile celebrities were being treated at UCLA, and yes, she was there when Michael Jackson died.

Our mutual multi-talent Page pal, Dinah Brein, continues to pursue her passion for music as a songwriter while also working in public relations. She lives in Seattle and visits us a few times a year with her husband, Larry (that is if they can find a dog sitter for their fur babies).

Jim McDonald decided to take a job away from NBC, where he quickly learned the ways of the Black Tower at Universal Studios. Soon, he was promoted to the executive position of Director of Current Television, overseeing shows including *Murder, She Wrote.*

Tom Hansen has had a long career in radio, which is no easy task. He worked as an owner and sales in the Los Angeles area for decades. He lives about forty-five minutes from Burbank, near fellow former Page Neil Weiner.

Tim Danker was able to stay at NBC longer than most of us, working in finance as a Unit Manager on daytime dramas and game shows, including *Wheel of Fortune.* He worked in theatre for many years, which was great because he could get us tickets to dozens of fabulous performances. Tim is the point person in our group who seamlessly coordinates most of our get-togethers, including a massive reunion on November 13, 1982, which we gratefully attended.

Brian Robinette, who earned a degree in Journalism from USC, fulfilled his goal by working in press and publicity for several decades. After retiring, he returned to NBC, working in the stressful corporate communications environment. He has since retired again and works as a freelance writer.

Beth Rees, and two other women on staff, left to start an audience service business, arranging tickets for groups to see shows taping around the city. That job was short-lived when Beth was awarded the opportunity to participate in the Directors Guild of America apprentice program.

Jeff Garrett worked as a location manager for TV shows, including *Beverly Hills, 90210,* and the films *Pineapple Express* and *Superbad. He* doesn't miss waking up earlier every day as he did for decades. He and his wife Gretchen spend half the year in California and the other half on the East coast enjoying their grandchildren.

Sandy (Crompton) Selma left the Page staff and the ticket department behind and became an international flight attendant for United Airlines.

She met her husband Reggie, a CNN White House cameraman, on a flight-and now they have two daughters.

George Glovna is semi-retired but still works a few days a month as an Asssociate News Director/Stage Manager. He reminded me of an adventure when Al Ovadia, Gregg Moscoe,and I piled into George's 70s Green Oldsmobile Cutlass and headed to Las Vegas to participate in the 1st (and perhaps only) Annual Tuber Olympics. We were all dressed up, and George recalled that as we walked through the MGM Casino, women gave themselves whiplash as Al strolled past the roulette tables. George turned to Al, who was oblivious to the attention, and said, "These women are checking you out but you're sharing a room with me tonight!" To this day, George sends a text to me on Harry Chapin's birthday.

With his eye still focused on working in the news arena, Pete Hammond, who remembers giving a total of 460 tours, became an award-winning awards analyst of film and television. On the way up the ladder of success, Pete produced stories on such diverse shows as *Entertainment Tonight, Extra, Access Hollywood, The Arsenio Hall Show, The Martin Short Show,* and the AMC Network. Pete is also a multi-Emmy nominated writer and often moderates television and motion picture events. In 1996 and again in 2013, Peter was awarded the Publicist Guild of America's Press Award, only the second journalist to be given this honor twice. His byline can be seen online on the must-read entertainment news site, Deadline.

Tommy Patino has spent his career working in television for over three decades as one of the producers on the NBC Rose Parade. For nearly ten years, he's been hired by The Academy of Television Arts and Sciences as a consultant in charge of their international broadcast. His job is to interface with twenty-five countries, including Armed Forces Television, to ensure they receive the Primetime Emmy Awards broadcast.

Al Ovadia married and became a father. He also became Executive Vice President, Consumer Products, managing worldwide licensing and international promotions. If you have any *Simpsons* merchandise at home, you can thank Al. Now, he is an artist specializing in pottery, really fabulous pottery!

A woman I briefly worked with as a Page, Cheri (Eichen) Steinkellner earned an Emmy and has been recognized as a Writer and Executive Producer on series including *Cheers*. Theatrically, she was nominated for a Tony Award for Best Book of a Musical for *Sister Act*.

A story I have to share with you comes from Marilee Mahoney. What you have to know about Marilee is she would literally give you the shirt off her back, which she did for me. She came to work one day wearing the most beautiful peach-colored silk blouse I'd ever seen. Honest to God, I had never seen a silk blouse. Remember, I worked at Sears. It was perfectly, stunningly, casually elegant. I complimented her on the blouse while we changed into our uniforms in the Subterranean Lounge. Marilee took it off, handed it to me, and said, "Here, you can have it." To this day, that's how kind and sincerely lovely a woman she is. And that's why her exit story is so naively genuine and heartwarming.

Marilee accepted a job within the walls of NBC, working in the Compliance and Practices Department. These employees ensure game shows are on the up-and-up, with no cheating. Marilee worked directly with Susan Simons, a former game show production assistant who had worked on various shows, including touring Bob Hope when he entertained the troops in Vietnam. Susan is still a dear friend who is organized and highly professional. Marilee lost her job within hours after it began in the most guileless way. Susan used the intercom to call Marilee into her office to "take a memo." Marilee, eager to please, responded, "Where would you like me to take it?" At that point, Susan shook her head and told Marilee, "This isn't going to work out." No joke. Marilee honestly didn't realize what Susan needed from her. Fortunately, Marilee found her way and became a trusted press agent for many of the day's top stars. Decades later, Marilee was recruited by NBC in New York to be their Manager of Press Relations. Now living in La Quinta, near Palm Springs, CA, Marilee says her time working as a Page was "the greatest job I had."

Tom Chasuk has remained my close friend all these years. His first job away from the Page staff was as a legal secretary. But soon after, he secured a Production Assistant position with *The Tomorrow Show*. Tom used that experience to land a job in New York as an Associate Producer on *The Morning Show,* hosted by Regis Philbin and Cyndy Garvey. That led to becoming the Producer of *Regis Philbin's Lifestyles.* He remained good friends with Regis after returning to California to work on the daytime series *AM Los Angeles.* It was there he had an only-in-Hollywood life-changing moment. At the last minute, a guest fell out of a segment on this live TV show. Tom came to the rescue, inventing a new persona for himself on the spot as The Bean Gourmet. He aced the cooking segment. Inspired to see where his fifteen minutes of fame would take him, he wrote a book that included a fantastic fudge recipe using beans and appeared on numerous talk shows, including *The Tonight Show with Jay Leno.* Leno's introduction included the nice tidbit that Tom was a former Page who had returned to his old touring grounds. Through the years, Tom and I have worked together at several radio stations in the Los Angeles area, and once on a New Year's Day, we co-hosted a three-hour show with our unique brand of gossip and giggles. I doubt management listened as we inmates took over the asylum for one glorious day with our guests: psychics and card readers, who made all sorts of wild predictions for the coming year. Almost an afterthought, Tom mentioned that in 1984, he sold two jokes to Joan Rivers. Her rate had increased since Linda and I sold her a few jokes. Joan was now paying $10 per joke and had Tom sign a contract where she retained all the rights to the material she bought from him.

Much to my dismay, I have lost touch with a few of my former colleagues. I've continued to try to locate one woman in particular. She had a great smile, was funny, extremely intelligent, and had an eating disorder. We didn't know about such things in the mid-seventies. Her family worried about her and hired a therapist to sit with her at lunch to help relieve her anxiety so she could eat. I bought a beautiful wood kitchen table from her when she moved back home to New York. I cherish it to this day and think of her often. I hope she's well and happy.

Over the last forty-plus years, a core group of us has remained a tight group of friends. We gather six to eight times a year to watch the award shows on TV, sporting events, and even election results. We have attended each other's birthday celebrations, weddings, and our parents' funerals. For more years than I can count, Pete and his Madelyn have continued their tradition of opening their home to us the Saturday before Christmas for a catered dinner that features authentic Chasen's Chili, lively conversation, games, and a gift exchange. The advent of technology, including Facetime and Zoom, has provided us with the opportunities to remain close to cherished Page Pals who no longer live near.

After all these decades, our circle of friends now includes the Page-in-Laws: the sweethearts and spouses of the OPs (Original Pages). Then we have the Page Adjacents: the ex-sweethearts, new spouses, and the children of the OPs.

Dinah met Steve Goldstein when she saw him listed as one of The 100 Most Eligible Bachelors in Los Angeles. And as Seinfeld's George Costanza might have put it, "yada yada yada," they dated for three years. Steve wrote, "Little did I know in 1983 that I was about to meet a group of people who would become like a second family to me for the rest of my life." Dinah arranged for Steve to be backstage at *The Tonight Show* on October 23, 1984, just as Paul McCartney was leaving the building. Steve handed Paul a photo of a church in Liverpool, McCartney's hometown, that he immediately recognized and acknowledged, giving Steve a brief once-in-a-lifetime brush with a Beatle to remember. He signed the photo, and then he was gone. Steve happily remembers, "We shared a moment."

I think Reggie, Sandy's husband, speaks for all the spouses who have had to listen to our stories countless times over the years. "One of the many joys of marrying my lovely wife, Sandy (Crompton) Selma, are my friendships and family-like bond with the original NBC Pages, of which she is a proud member." So, thank you for being a friend, Audrey Bamber, Daryl Busby, Randall Carver, Jennifer & Steve Goldstein (and numerous children and grandchildren), Madelyn Hammond, Melissa Hellyar-Mersch and Trevor Mersch, Todd Moster, Larry McClellan, Kathleen Swanson, Evan Swanson, Michele Walsh, and Linda Wilkes.

On December 21, 2012, I married one of the most handsome, talented, and patient men in the world, Randall Carver. Randall is an actor best remembered for starring in the TV series *Taxi* and appearing in films including *Midnight Cowboy*, *Time to Run*, and *There Will Be Blood*. We had a cute meet. I was hoping to find a home for a stray dog. Randy adopted the gorgeous sixty-pound red-haired mixed-breed boy with the constant smile he named Rocco. About six months later, I met Randy and offered to dog-sit. Little did I know, Randy traveled to Texas frequently to visit his ailing mother, and Rocco needed a lot of care. I would live at Randy's home for months at a time until our romance blossomed. We never really dated. We just kind of fell into each other's arms and have been holding on tight since our first night together. Randy was immediately welcomed into Pagedom. "I'd never been around a group of entertainment friends who had so many parties, so many stories, and now, I'm included as part of the family. The Pages always have each other's backs. How blessed they are to have found each other."

My journey through the biz has been a bit circuitous. I worked days as a secretary and joined an improv comedy group by night. I intended to learn improv techniques to help me become a better writer. The skills came in handy when I was spotted by someone in the audience of our show and was quickly cast on a segment of NBC's *TV's Bloopers and Practical Jokes,* where I played a reporter punking Billy Dee Williams at a restaurant he owned on Melrose Ave. It was my first union acting job, my first TV credit, and, best of all, it was an NBC show. That led to starring on the syndicated comedy series *Off the Wall* and HBO's *Night Rap.* From there, I worked as an actor on the syndicated series *Candid Camera.* It was a fantastic job that allowed me to travel around the country, pranking people and seeing how genuinely happy they were when they were told to "Smile. You're on *Candid Camera.*" The job did get a bit tricky as some people would get wise to the ridiculous situations we'd put them in. The producers told us to cuss if "the mark" suspected they were being taped on a hidden camera. I made more than a few people blush when I'd reply, "No fucking way you're on *Candid Camera,*" so we could save the set-up and use parts of it on the show.

I was beyond excited to be cast as one of the stars of a game show/comedy pilot titled *Show Me*. It was taped in Studio 3, where I saw a new generation of Pages ushering an audience, this time to see me perform! I've acted on many shows, done voiceovers, hosted eight infomercials, and even ran a teleprompter to earn extra money. For some unexplained reason (perhaps it was my form-fitting red jumpsuit), I got a job co-hosting *Battle of the Monster Trucks and Mud Bog Spectacular* for ESPN. I received an Emmy nomination as a Writer for the daytime series *Breakaway,* but I lost. I recall the awards ceremony fondly because it was officially the first time I introduced Randall as my boyfriend to my colleagues.

I've been able to pick up work in the game show field, one of the most fun being *Supermarket Sweep*. I had a staff writing job for the NBC game show *Million Second Quiz*. I was even one of the three "Phone A Friend" friends of *Batman* star Adam West when he appeared with Regis Philbin on *Who Wants to Be a Millionaire?* I co-starred on an episode of the short-lived NBC series, *Sunnyside,* where I had a scene with Kal Penn. Seeing my name in the credits nearly forty years after starting my career at NBC felt especially special. Oh, and I became a published non-fiction writer.

I may not have known what I was doing. I just knew I wanted to do it. Becoming an NBC Page changed my life, all for the better. The friendships I made, the experiences we had, and the history we witnessed became life lessons we have taken into the real world. My Page friends are a resourceful group who have always been there for each other. Without their stories and our showbiz kinship, I couldn't have done this book. We have always been each other's best cheerleaders. I have always believed you should walk in the footsteps of where you want to be. As I often tell my husband, "Fixate on Flexibility." Try not to get only one way of achieving your goals stuck in your head. Find a way to fit into the life you want.

If I'm determined to get a job, I start by working backward to create a path to my ultimate success. I learn what it will take to get where I want to be. That's what I did to eventually become the Head Writer of a TV show where I earned an Emmy nomination. I lied my ass off and said

I knew how to use a new computer system installed in the offices of a daily talk show, and I got the job! The weekend before I began, I immersed myself in all things computer as my patient friend showed me everything from turning on the machine to printing a final document. Monday morning, I was ready, except when I got to my desk, I realized I had learned a vastly different operating system. Thankfully, while the rest of the staff sat behind closed doors all day assigning producers to segments, I hunted and pecked my way through the keyboard and figured out how to format and save a script. I knew the show inside and out and, a few months later, noticed no one had been assigned a script needed for the pre-tape of the Thanksgiving show. I offered to write the Thanksgiving show for free. I worked after-hours and in-between my almost nonexistent down-time during the day. It took me three days, but I did it! A few weeks later, a writer didn't renew his contract, so I asked to interview for the position, emphasizing my knowledge of all aspects of the show and how I could jump in, making for a smooth transition. Getting the script typist job-a job I didn't really want, but needed to reach my goal, led to my goal of becoming a staff writer, and I was able to qualify for my Writers Guild Card! And when another writer quit, I became the Head Writer. I went from lowly script typist to Head Writer in one year.

Many years ago, at a Writers Guild event, I had the opportunity to hear author Ray Bradbury speak to a room full of aspiring writers. Someone in the room asked Bradbury how he knew if what he was writing was any good or not. Bradbury responded, "Think with your gut. Your heart and your head will always try to justify a situation. But your gut will always tell you the truth." Simply put, trust your instinct. That not only applies to your creativity, but it's also a good life lesson when presented with opportunities that seem too good to be true.

Remember, luck can happen when preparation meets opportunity. You don't have to know everything. Be willing to listen and learn and show up ready to hit the ground running. Let people know you're dependable. And, if you're ready, really, really, ready to make a first impression, find a way to make yourself known in a way people can't wait to meet you. Be consistent and persistent. Read as much as you can about the people you want to meet. See if you have any connection to them that you can mention in a cover letter or chat. Maybe you went to the same university, or you both volunteer at the same organization? If one door closes, knock on more doors, and find a way to meet the people key to your next opportunity. Make your next adventure an exhilarating trip outside your comfort zone. Put yourself out there. Take a chance. It's never too late to be the person you always wanted to grow up to be.

EPILOGUE

By mid-September 2022, I had finished writing this manuscript. I began the process of proofreading, and I apologize now if you've spotted a few oopsies. I approached this project from a place of love and fun with the goal of chronicling our cherished times at NBC Burbank. Surprisingly, some unresolved feelings were stirred-up, and a little voice in my head started questioning if I should look for a publisher or just copy the manuscript on a flash drive and stick it in a drawer.

Then, something happened on September 17, 2022, that sent my head spinning.

I spent that Saturday morning at my friend Susan's home for our neighborhood's annual Garage Sale. I brought a few items and put them on display, hoping not to return home with them. A neatly dressed man stopped by who didn't look as slovenly as the neighborhood lookie-loos. He eyed a few items, then walked away.

An hour later, he returned, and we chatted about the vintage figurines I was selling. We began talking about the historic events unfolding over the weekend surrounding the funeral of Queen Elizabeth II. I told him I had the opportunity to be at the Queen's 25th Jubilee. He said he was, also, and remarked about the pageantry and fly-over at Buckingham Palace. "What a small world!" I said, "We were in the same crowd forty-six years ago." He mentioned how hot it was, and I recalled our tour bus stopping at several restaurants hoping to get ice for our drinks. He said his bus did the same thing. I asked where he stayed in London, and it was The Kensington Hilton, where I also had a room. I then looked at him, almost knowing the answer before I asked, "What airline did you fly on the way home?" He said, "Pan Am," and in unison, we said, "And a man died on the plane on the way home."

The man I met had been a doctor on my flight! He told me he had been in the first class section, up the spiral staircase, when he heard the flight attendant's announcement. He remembered standing next to another doctor, a dermatologist when red hair and pale skin, while some firefighters tended to the man. Yep, that was Dr. Korn, the red-haired man I mentioned in the first chapter of this book! I wanted to be certain that I heard correctly, so I asked if he remembered where we made an emergency landing. He said, "Nova Scotia," then quickly corrected himself and said, "No, it was Goose Bay, Labrador. Then we landed in Chicago three-hours later." There was now no doubt about it. We were on the same flight!

We both stopped and looked at each other, a bit incredulous. I extended my hand, introducing myself, as I do, to the doctor. I won't mention his name here but know he is a respected psychiatrist in the San Fernando Valley area in Los Angeles.

Why was this man who didn't look like the other neighbors rummaging through my tchotchkes? I was compelled to call his office Monday morning. I said, "You never asked for my name or telephone number, but if you've been thinking about our meeting each other as much as I have, you should have my contact information." He said he was with his IT guy and had just "told him my...I mean, our story." He also informed me he researched Dr. Korn only to learn he had passed away several years ago. A few days later, I sent a note to the last known address of his widow, but the post office returned it to me as undelivered. I wanted to tell her our story.

I'm a very practical thinker. So when this woo-woo (what are the odds of this kind of moment happening) happened, I needed to take a few days to process why I met the doctor when I did. I finally figured out the why. Whatever insecurities I harbored about publishing my stories and the stories of my friends were now gone. I was exactly where I was supposed to be forty-six years ago and that day at the garage sale. I saw it as a sign that I should publish this book. My life had come full circle.

Yup. Harry Chapin was right.

All my life's a circle; But I can't tell you why; Season's spinning round again; The years keep rollin' by.

LIST OF TITLES, IN ALPHABETICAL ORDER

My Peacock Tale: Secrets Of An NBC Page

A Family Upside Down (1978)

Access Hollywood (1996)

Adam (1983)

All-Star Review (1952)

AM Los Angeles (1975)

Annie (Live Theater) (1976)

Anything For Money (1984)

Back To The Future (1985)

Battle of the Monster Trucks and Mud Bog Spectacular (1988)

Beverly Hills, 90210 (1990)

Blue Hawaii (1961)

Bob Hope Comedy Specials (1963)

Breakaway (1984)

Buck Rogers in 25th Century (1979)

Candid Camera (1948)

Captain Kangaroo (1955)

Car Wash (1976)

Catch-22 (1970)

Celebrity Sweepstakes (1974)

Cheers (1982)

Chico and the Man (1974)

ChiPs (1977)

CPO Sharkey (1976)

Days of Our Lives (1965)

Dick Clark's Live Wednesday (1978)

Diff'rent Strokes (1978)

Ellery Queen (1975)

Empty Nest (1988)

Entertainment Tonight (1981)

Extra (1994)

Extreme Gong (1998)

Family (1976)

Family Feud (1976)

Family Plot (1976)

Fred Allen Radio Show (1932)

Grindl (1963)

Hanky Panky (1982)

High Rollers (1974)

Hogan's Heroes (1965)

Hollywood Squares (1965)

How's Your Mother-in-Law (1967)

I Love Lucy (1951)

In The Ghetto (1969)

It's Always Something (Book) (2009)

Jaws (1975)

Johnny Cash Special (1977)

Lady Sings the Blues (1972)

Late Night with Seth Meyers (2014)

Let's Make A Deal (1963)

M*A*S*H (1972)

Magnum, PI (1980)

Man on the Moon (1999)

Meet the Press (1947)

Melrose Place (1992)

Midnight Cowboy (1969)

Million Second Quiz (2013)

Models, Inc (1994)

Murder, She Wrote (1984)

NBC Nightly News (1970)

NBC's TV's Bloopers and Practical Jokes (1984)

Night Rap (1990)

Off The Wall (1986)

Password (1961)

Pineapple Express (2008)

Police Academy (1984)

Pretty Woman (1990)

Psycho (1960)

Real People (1979)

Regis Philbin's Lifestyles (1984)

Ringo (1978)

Rowan & Martin;s Laugh-In (1967)

Ryan's Hope (1975)

Sanford and Son (1972)

Saturday Night Fever (1977)

Saturday Night Live (1975)

Saved By the Bell (1989)

Sea Hunt (1961)

Silver Streak (1976)

Sister Act (Live Performance) (2011)

Star Wars (1977)

Stop the Wheel, I Want to Get Off (Book) (2010)

Sunnyside (2019)

Superbad (2007)

Supermarket Sweep (1990)

Surprise Gardner (1998)

Sybil (1976)

Taxi (1978)

The Arsenio Hall Show (1989)

The Bob Newhart Show (1972)

The Boy in the Plastic Bubble (1976)

The Carol Burnett Show (1967)

The Cosby Show (1984)

The Courtship of Eddie's Father (1969)

The Dating Game (1965)

The Doris Day Show (1968)

The Ed Sullivan Show (1948)

The Gong Show (1976)

The Gong Show Movie (1980)

The Harvey Korman Show (1977)

The Last Great Ride (Book) (1992)

The Late Show Starring Joan Rivers (1986)

The Liar's Club (1976)

The Love Boat (1977)

The Martin Short Show (1994)

The McLean Stevenson Show (1976)

The Merv Griffin Show (1962)

The Midnight Special (1972)

The Mike Douglas Show (1961)

The Morning Show (1983)

The New Treasure Hunt (1972)

The Newlywed Game (1966)

The Richard Pryor Show (1977)

The Rocky Horror Show (Live Theater) (1974)

The Simpsons (1989)

The Steve Allen Plymouth Show (1951)

The Thornbirds (1983)

The Today Show (1952)

The Tomorrow Show (1973)

The Tonight Show Starring Jimmy Fallon (2014)

The Tonight Show Starring Johnny Carson (1962)

The Tonight Show with Jay Leno (1992)

The Trouble With Angels (1966)

The Twilight Zone (1959)

The Walton's (1972)

The Wild, Wild West (1965)

There Will Be Blood (2007)

Time to Run (1973)

Totally Hidden Video (1989)

Tournament of Roses Parade (1954)

Trump Card (1990)

Truth of Consequences (1950)

Van Dyke and Company (1975)

Viva Las Vegas (1964)

Welcome Back, Kotter (1975)

Wheel of Fortune (1975)

Who Wants to Be A Millionaire (2013)

Yahtzee (1988)

You Don't Say (1963)

Your Show of Shows (1950)

2001: A Space Odyssey (1968)

3's A Crowd (1979)

50 Grand Slam (1976)

BIBLIOGRAPHY

ANDY KAUFMAN:

https://www.britannica.com/biography/Andy-Kaufman

https://www.imdb.com/title/tt0074068/

https://www.imdb.com/name/nm0001412/?ref_=fn_al_nm_1

https://www.mentalfloss.com/article/75669/when-andy-kaufman-lost-it-live-television

https://www.youtube.com/watch?v=Yxp23Gkvn9g

https://faroutmagazine.co.uk/andy-kaufman-banned-snl-reason-saturday-night-live/

https://www.huffpost.com/entry/remembering-andy-kaufman-_b_5332029

https://www.thelist.com/441148/the-real-reason-andy-kaufman-was-banned-from-snl/

https://www.imdb.com/name/nm0000120/?ref_=fn_al_nm_1

http://www.thestudiotour.com/paramount/stage23.php

CHINESE THEATRE:

http://www.tclchinesetheatres.com/about-us/

CHUCK BARRIS:

https://www.youtube.com/watch?v=qNsE1_tRrrY

https://ringostrack.com/en/movie/the-gong-show-movie/47612

https://www.youtube.com/watch?v=qOR8YJJR0d8

https://www.today.com/popculture/barris-excess-killed-my-daughter-2D80556363

https://www.findagrave.com/memorial/98249657/della-charlotte-barris

https://www.imdb.com/title/tt0133303/?ref_=fn_al_tt_1

https://www.imdb.com/name/nm0001320/bio?ref_=nm_ov_bio_sm

https://outsider.com/news/entertainment/the-gong-show-premieres-on-this-day-1976/

https://www.imdb.com/name/nm0546439/?ref_=nv_sr_srsg_0

https://en.wikipedia.org/wiki/The_Gong_Show

https://groovyhistory.com/gong-celebrities-steve-martin-pee-wee-herman

https://en.wikipedia.org/wiki/The_Gong_Show_Movie

https://www.imdb.com/title/tt0080808/?ref_=fn_al_tt_1

https://www.google.com/search?q=steve+martin+gong+show&sxsrf=ALeKk027ruYdPIhSeBKjsVYyWj44w10vxg%3A1628999051021&source=hp&ei=io0YYfvsO5Ot0PEPh_KV4A0&iflsig=AINFCbYAAAAAYRibmx2Gr1VvWS9XQxZFPdmNO5-ga7XP&oq=steve+martin&gs_lcp=-Cgdnd3Mtd2l6EAEYADIECCMQJzILCC4QgAQQsQMQgwEyCwgAE-IAEELEDEIMBMgsIABCABBCxAxCDATILCAAQgAQQsQMQgwEyC-wgAEIAEELEDEIMBMg4IABCABBCxAxCDARCLAzIICAAQgAQQi-wMyFAguEIAEELEDEIMBEIsDEKMDEKgDMg4IABCABBCxAxC-DARCLAzoKCC4Q6gIQJxCTAjoHCCMQ6gIQJzoECC4QQQzo-ICAAQgAQQsQM6DgguEIAEELEDEMcBEKMCOgUILhCRAjoKC-C4QxwEQrwEQQzoLCC4QgAQQxwEQowI6CAguEIAEELEDOgQ-IABBDOgcILhCxAxBDOggILhCxAxCDAToLCAAQgAQQsQMQiwM-6CwgAELEDEIMBEIsDOhQILhCABBCxAxCDARCLAxCoAxCjA1D-2CVj1G2DALWgBcAB4AIABfIgB_QmSAQMzLjmYAQCgAQGwAQq-4AQM&sclient=gws-wiz

https://www.today.com/popculture/barris-excess-killed-my-daughter-2D80556363

https://www.imdb.com/find?q=danny+elfman&ref_=nv_sr_sm

https://en.wikipedia.org/wiki/Chuck_Barris

https://www.metv.com/lists/11-gong-worthy-facts-about-the-gong-show

https://www.metv.com/lists/11-gong-worthy-facts-about-the-gong-show

https://www.imdb.com/title/tt0133303/?ref_=fn_al_tt_1

https://www.usatoday.com/picture-gallery/life/2017/03/22/game-show-king-chuck-barris-1929-2017/99485362/

https://www.imdb.com/name/nm0666565/bio?ref_=nm_ov_bio_sm

https://www.hollywoodreporter.com/news/general-news/chuck-barris-dead-gong-show-929310/

https://www.youtube.com/watch?v=5WGklfKprf0

https://www.youtube.com/watch?v=qOR8YJJR0d8 – Chuck's long interview

https://heavy.com/entertainment/2017/03/chuck-barris-dead-obituary-cause-wife-family-gong-show-cia-daughter-age/

https://www.youtube.com/watch?v=WCjOtdyUB-I

https://variety.com/2017/tv/news/chuck-barris-dead-dies-gong-show-host-1202013790/

https://www.washingtonpost.com/news/morning-mix/wp/2017/03/22/chuck-barris-host-of-the-gong-show-who-wildly-claimed-to-be-a-cia-assassin-dead-at-87/

https://dailyentertainmentnews.com/breaking-news/chuck-barris-wives-girlfriends-children/

DAVID BRENNER:

https://www.youtube.com/watch?v=N0kev4QV2aY

https://www.imdb.com/title/tt0400028/?ref_=fn_al_tt_1

DELLA REESE:

https://people.com/archive/near-death-after-her-collapse-on-the-tonight-show-della-reese-is-singing-again-but-not-the-blues-vol-13-no-20/

https://www.youtube.com/watch?v=M8hfse64sFU

https://www.imdb.com/name/nm0005343/?ref_=fn_al_nm_1

https://lfpress.com/2017/11/20/della-reese-once-saved-by-londons-dr-charles-drake-has-died

DONALD TRUMP:

https://www.thedailybeast.com/ivana-trump-recounts-the-donalds-public-affair-with-marla-maples

https://www.curbed.com/2021/01/nyc-aims-to-end-the-wollman-contract-that-built-trumps-myth.html

https://apnews.com/article/marla-maples-north-america-donald-trump-ap-top-news-celebrities-9d635fbd5b4d4998a7938dd9596759f7

https://www.biography.com/us-president/donald-trump

FLOYD JACKSON:

https://www.latimes.com/archives/la-xpm-1989-09-04-me-1133-story.html

https://www.youtube.com/watch?v=6ud6o5WEYAQ

FORMER NBC PAGES:

Richard Benjamin - https://www.imdb.com/name/nm0000907/?ref_=fn_al_nm_1

Aubrey Plaza - https://www.imdb.com/name/nm2201555/?ref_=fn_al_nm_1

Hugh Downs - https://www.imdb.com/name/nm0236180/?ref_=fn_al_nm_1

Regis Philbin - https://www.imdb.com/name/nm0005310/?ref_=fn_al_nm_1

Peter Marshall - https://www.imdb.com/name/nm0551102/?ref_=fn_al_nm_1

Chuck Barris - https://www.imdb.com/find?q=chuck+barris&ref_=nv_sr_sm

https://en.wikipedia.org/wiki/NBC_page

FRANK SINATRA:

https://www.imdb.com/name/nm0000069/?ref_=fn_al_nm_1

https://www.biography.com/musician/frank-sinatra

FREDDIE PRINZE:

https://www.latimes.com/local/obituaries/archives/la-me-freddie-prinz-19770130-story.html

https://www.drugs.com/illicit/quaaludes.html

https://www.imdb.com/name/nm0697905/?ref_=fn_al_nm_1

https://findadeath.com/freddie-prinze/

https://www.vulture.com/2017/02/freddie-prinze-tonight-show.html

https://www.imdb.com/name/nm0464506/?ref_=fn_al_nm_1

https://www.findagrave.com/memorial/839/freddie-prinze

https://stowens.medium.com/the-prinze-of-comedy-91676dbcd3de

https://reelreviews.com/shorttakes/prinze.htm

https://www.hazeldenbettyford.org/about-us/history

https://www.youtube.com/watch?v=BfPZnnIxN38

GARY GILMORE:

http://www.clarkprosecutor.org/html/death/US/gilmore001.htm

https://www.nga.org/governor/scott-m-matheson/

https://www.abc4.com/news/justice-files/the-justice-files-the-execution-of-gary-gilmore-2/

https://archive.sltrib.com/article.php?id=58166113&itype=cmsid

GENE PATTON (GENE GENE THE DANCING MACHINE):

https://heavy.com/news/2015/03/gene-gene-the-dancing-machine-gene-patton-eugene-the-gong-show-dead-diabetes-chuck-barris-confessions-of-a-dangerous-mind/

https://www.newsfromme.com/2015/03/25/remembering-gene/

GENE WOOD:

https://www.imdb.com/name/nm0939712/?ref_=ttfc_fc_cl_t320

GILDA RADNER:

https://www.goodreads.com/author/quotes/145047.Gilda_Radner

https://www.gettyimages.com/photos/gilda-radner-honored-by-the-hollywood-walk-of-fame

https://www.gildasclubqc.org/about-us/history/

https://www.findagrave.com/memorial/848/gilda-radner

https://www.biography.com/performer/gilda-radner

https://gesmithmusic.com/

https://www.imdb.com/name/nm0705717/?ref_=nv_sr_srsg_0

https://www.youtube.com/watch?v=9hYGtXIqDa0

https://www.imdb.com/name/nm0705717/bio

https://www.britannica.com/biography/Gilda-Radner

https://www.youtube.com/results?search_query=lisa+loopner+and+todd

https://www.yahoo.com/lifestyle/tagged/health/tv-news/a-brief-history-of-barbara-walters-s-nickname--baba-wawa-202447087.html

https://www.imdb.com/name/nm0084642/?ref_=fn_al_nm_1

HARVEY KORMAN:

https://www.imdb.com/title/tt0207887/?ref_=nm_flmg_act_5333

JAY MICHELIS:

Adam Movie: https://www.imdb.com/title/tt0085136/?ref_=nm_flmg_act_43

https://www.latimes.com/archives/la-xpm-1988-09-12-mn-1204-story.html

https://www.latimes.com/archives/la-xpm-1988-09-23-me-2709-story.html

https://www.orlandosentinel.com/

https://books.google.com/books?id=suS8CwAAQBAJ&pg=PT146&lpg=PT146&dq=jay+michelis&source=bl&ots=RXKLtQzcBw&sig=ACfU3U2YxeBDcPwh_bwtNtkk4GfPtX0ETA&hl=en&sa=X&ved=2ahUKEwii0_m9ntXyAhW8IDQIHZFCAYwQ6AF6BAgWEAM#v=onepage&q=jay%20michelis&f=false

https://ew.com/tv/2018/02/16/joan-rivers-johnny-carson-feud-interview/

https://people.com/celebrity/joan-rivers-and-johnny-carsons-history-on-the-tonight-show/

https://www.biography.com/news/joan-rivers-johnny-carson-feud

https://www.biography.com/news/joan-rivers-johnny-carson-feud
https://www.primetimer.com/watch/johnny-carson-announced-his-
     retirement-30-years-ago-today

JOAN RIVERS:

https://www.nytimes.com/2016/11/28/books/review/joan-rivers-
     biography-last-girl-before-freeway-leslie-bennetts.html
https://www.vogue.com/article/joan-rivers-last-girl-before-freeway-
     leslie-bennetts-interview
https://www.biography.com/performer/joan-rivers
https://buffalonews.com/entertainment/books/probing-the-reasons-
     for-rivers-need-to-work-anger-later-in-her-life/article_d6c4a566-
     3406-5963-a12e-0846ac1af51c.html.

JOE NAMATH:

https://www.pro-football-reference.com/players/N/NamaJo00.htm

MARILEE MAHONEY:

https://medium.com/@bchew.boldpointnow/secrets-of-hollywood-
     crime-pays-when-mahoney-is-talking-3905a6257c4a
https://www.latimes.com/archives/la-xpm-2005-jun-08-me-tebet8-
     story.html

McLEAN STEVENSON:

https://www.imdb.com/name/nm0829004/bio
https://www.nytimes.com/1996/02/17/arts/mclean-stevenson-dies-at-
     66-star-of-tv-s-m-a-s-h-series.html
https://live.autographmagazine.com/forum/topics/need-advice?xg_
     source=activity
https://entertainment.howstuffworks.com/question443.htm

MEET THE PRESS:

https://www.imdb.com/title/tt0149490/

MIDNIGHT SPECIAL:

https://en.wikipedia.org/wiki/Wolfman_Jack

https://en.wikipedia.org/wiki/Bay_City_Rollers

https://www.youtube.com/watch?v=_QpdmBxIrvM

https://www.youtube.com/watch?v=CL7t22rypew

https://www.usnews.com/news/special-reports/articles/2014/01/22/
video-the-beatles-on-the-ed-sullivan-show-feb-9-1964#:~:text=
22%2C%202014%2C%20at%203%3A25%20p.m.&text=The%20
Beatles%20were%20already%20a,minute%20break%20for%20
other%20performers.

http://www.personalmanagershalloffame.org/jeff-wald.html

Bay City Rollers: https://youtu.be/FrkNoWIho_M https://www.imdb.
com/title/tt0076666/?ref_=fn_al_tt_1

MRS. MILLER:

https://www.imdb.com/name/nm2181640/bio?ref_=nm_ov_bio_sm

NBC CHIMES

http://www.old-time.com/misc/chimes.html

https://en.wikipedia.org/wiki/NBC_chimes

https://www.latimes.com/archives/la-xpm-1985-12-12-mn-16152-story.
html

NBC PAGE PROGRAM – CURRENT:

https://www.youtube.com/watch?v=gB_VE5hCN7E

https://www.businessinsider.com/this-job-more-selective-than-navy-
seals-2016-6

https://corporate.comcast.com/news-information/news-feed/nbcun
iversals-page-program-80-years-of-historic-moments

https://www.today.com/allday/makeover-nbc-page-program-gets-new-
look-8c10989154

NIPPER:

https://www.rca.com/us_en/nipper-chipper-1720-us-en

OPERATION MEND:

https://veterans.ucla.edu/services/operation-mend

RALPH ANDREWS:

https://www.newspapers.com/clip/39996186/yahtzee-2/
https://casetext.com/case/ralph-andrews-productions-v-paramount-
   pictures
https://en.wikipedia.org/wiki/Yahtzee_(game_show)
https://www.imdb.com/title/tt0198053/fullcredits/?ref_=tt_cl_sm
https://en.wikipedia.org/wiki/Totally_Hidden_Video

REDD FOXX:

https://www.imdb.com/name/nm0289359/?ref_=fn_al_nm_1

REGIS PHILBIN:

https://www.guinnessworldrecords.com/world-records/most-hours-
   on-us-television

RICHARD PRYOR:

https://www.youtube.com/watch?v=IoHxBmstE-I
https://www.imdb.com/name/nm0600520/?ref_=fn_al_nm_1
https://www.imdb.com/title/tt0075567/episodes?season=1&ref_=tt_
   eps_sn_1
https://www.biography.com/performer/richard-pryor

SALE OF NBC:

https://variety.com/2019/film/news/warner-bros-burbank-expansion-
   buildings-1203189703/?fbclid=IwAR1VyqnHk4B4-tjmgl0MxduHv65
   bmjxGQApZKvyj8gNGxz2hQkLAZZT25LU

SALLY FIELD:

https://www.imdb.com/title/tt0075296/?ref_=fn_al_tt_1

SUSAN STAFFORD:

https://www.amazon.com/Stop-Wheel-Want-Get-Off/dp/1436375290/
ref=sr_1_1?dchild=1&keywords=susan+Stafford&qid=1627579515
&sr=8-1

https://www.identitynetwork.net/apps/articles/default.asp?articleid=
50511&columnid=

TONIGHT SHOW:

https://www.facebook.com/rory.oconnor.7503/videos/102242006
13225832

https://elkhornvalleymuseum.org/discover/johnny-carson/

https://www.youtube.com/watch?v=Y5wU7SmkZ3U

https://www.primetimer.com/watch/johnny-carson-announced-his-
retirement-30-years-ago-today

https://thecomicscomic.com/2013/01/02/looking-for-the-big-laugh-
with-professor-ritch-shydner-two-jokes-over-the-line/

https://groovyhistory.com/tonight-show-guest-hosts

https://distancecalculator.globefeed.com/US_Distance_Result.asp?stat
e=CA&vr=apes&fromplace=3000%20W%20Alameda%20Ave,%20
#W,%20Burbank,%20CA,%2091523,%20USA&toplace=Point%20
Dume,%20CA,%20USA

https://www.youtube.com/watch?v=6ZZBJ7DawYw

https://www.biography.com/news/joan-rivers-johnny-carson-feud

http://www.steveallen.com/main_page/index.html

https://www.youtube.com/watch?v=pqGj5Bi77jg

https://www.legacy.com/news/johnny-carson-and-the-tonight-
show/

https://www.vanityfair.com/hollywood/2014/02/johnny-carson-the-
tonight-show

https://theaxisofego.com/2014/02/03/the-tonight-shows-forgotten-
host/

https://www.vanityfair.com/hollywood/2014/02/johnny-carson-the-
tonight-show

https://historygarage.com/heres-johnny-everything-tonight-shows-30-year-host-johnny-carson/3/

https://www.vogue.com/article/regis-philbin-dies-at-88-who-wants-to-be-a-millionaire

https://www.docseverinsen.com/about/

https://www.hollywoodreporter.com/tv/tv-news/shelly-cohen-dead-johnny-carsons-longtime-tonight-show-assistant-musical-director-was-84-1131977/

http://www.reddfoxx.com/

https://www.rollingstone.com/culture/culture-features/johnny-carson-the-rolling-stone-interview-45826/

https://www.biography.com/performer/johnny-carson

https://burbankinfocus.org/islandora/object/islandora%3A1461

https://www.youtube.com/watch?v=RiCwfw6RBgY

https://www.thedailybeast.com/i-was-there-inside-joan-rivers-funeral

https://www.latimes.com/archives/la-xpm-1986-05-07-ca-3848-story.html

Ricky Carson: https://apnews.com/article/af9ec01452f78be7d1a2500aa5497522

https://www.deseret.com/1991/7/19/18931532/tearful-carson-shares-grief-and-pride-in-his-son-s-eulogy

https://fabiosa.com/ctent-rsafr-auimk-pbimk-phakl-most-difficult-moment-of-my-life-johnny-carson-barely-survived-the-sudden-passing-of-his-son-in-1991/

Peter Lassally: https://www.cbsnews.com/news/peter-lassally-a-late-night-life/

TOTIE FIELDS:

https://en.wikipedia.org/wiki/Totie_Fields

https://www.thefamouspeople.com/profiles/totie-fields-3087.php#:~:text=Totie%20Fields%20was%20an%20American%20stand-up%20comedian.%20She,at%20Boston%20clubs%20from%20the%20age%20of%2020

THE TROUBLE WITH ANGELS:

https://www.imdb.com/title/tt0061122/?ref_=fn_al_tt_1

INDEX

www.ingramcontent.com/pod-product-compliance
Lightning Source LLC
Chambersburg PA
CBHW070753160726
48004CB00001B/169